THIRTY DAYS TO TRANSFORM YOURSELF

Tested and Proven Strategies of Transformation

By Dr. Iona German, PhD

Copyright © 2016 by Dr. Iona German, PhD

All rights reserved. This book or any portion thereof may not be reproduced or used in any manner whatsoever without the express written permission of the publisher except for the use of brief quotations in a book review.

Printed in the United States of America

First Printing, 2016

ISBN: 978-0-997-7682-0-6

All Thrive Global, LLC

2805 E Oakland Park Blvd #398

Fort Lauderdale, FL 33306

PERSONAL ACKNOWLEDGEMENTS

A special thank you to my family for affording me the time to author this book. Thanks to Latoya in New York for consenting to be mentioned in this book. A special gratitude to all my clients who through the years has allowed me to look into their lives.

My gratitude to all those who helped me to make this a reality and all credit to our wonderful Creator for wisdom, knowledge and understanding.

Dr Iona German, PhD

Lauderhill, Florida

June 2016.

INTRODUCTION

I am looking back at how and why this book all started! It was about 20 years ago when I was working two jobs, hosting my own Radio Show and found time to Counsel my clients, then I came to the reality that I could not make everybody happy overworking myself. My body was signaling me that it needed attention especially when I ate late and my stomach was disgruntled! My daughter was in her teenage years and my son wasn't fully ten years old, so my attention was very needed. My clientele had increased and everything was breaking loose!

I was also working among some folks who were very negative. Most of my income was coming from that negative environment. I would always talk positively to motivate my co-workers but to no avail. Then, I decided to change that negative environment regardless of the income. When I shared my decision with some of my co-workers, they would have every reason as to why I needed to stay there and not lost that income. I tuned them out of my subconscious mind so that I did not hear any repetition of their negatives.

I took a week off from work and wrote down all the positives and how I hoped to accomplish them. I made up a thirty days to transform yourself plan. I challenged myself and within thirty days, I started a full consultation practice. I had some of my clients to implement the "Thirty Days to Transform Yourself" and their lives changed for the better. I started to put the manuscript together and was almost finished when my computer burnt up. I kept on using the same formula to assist some of my clients who were willing to give it a try and they were satisfied.

One of my clients, Latoya M. was very terrified to quit a job that was very stressful. I used the same methods into this book and not only did she quit that stressful job, she is now a nurse and is still improving!

This book, "Thirty Days to Transform Yourself" has practical exercises for anyone who is willing to try these tested and proven strategies of transformation.

Dr. Iona German, PHD

TABLE OF CONTENTS

PERSONAL ACKNOWLEDGEMENTS iii
INTRODUCTION v
DAY 1: POSITIVE AFFIRMATIONS TO SELF 1
    Identifying negative internal chatter 3
    Implanting Positive Affirmations 3
    When feeling lonely 4
    When you are feeling terrified without any danger in sight 4
    When it seems like you don't matter 5
    When you are afraid 5
    When you are angry 5
    When you feel like all hope is lost 6
    When you can't make up your mind about a decision 6
    When you are with friends 6
DAY 2: IMPROVE YOUR SELF-ESTEEM 9
    1. Silence your inner critic 10
    2. Don't compare your life to that of other people 11
    3. Learn to handle mistakes and failures more positively 11
    4. Do something different 11
    5. Be kinder to others 12
    6. Spend more time with people who support you 12
DAY 3: BREAK A BAD HABIT 15
    What's responsible for bad habits? 15
    You replace a bad habit, you can't remove it 16
    Select a replacement for your undesirable habit 16
    Reduce the triggers as much as you can 17
    Watch out for the urges, and delay for as long as possible. 17
    Tell a friend or relative 17

    See yourself succeeding 18
    Ditch the people who make you engage in your old ways 18
    Factor in Failure 18
DAY 4: FIND YOUR LIFE'S PURPOSE 21
    1. Ask yourself, what kind of activities do I not get tired of? 22
    2. Ask yourself, what is it I really want to do but I'm scared of? .. 23
    3. Ask yourself, how can I help people? 24
DAY 5: LEARN TO HANDLE REJECTION NICELY 25
    1. Acknowledge rejection 25
    2. Treat yourself with compassion 26
    3. Don't take rejection personally 26
    4. Engage yourself in something else 26
    5. See rejection as a challenge 27
    6. Learn from it 27
    7. Don't let rejection affect your future 27
DAY 6: UNDERSTAND AND MANAGE SELF-CONTROL 29
    1. Make a list of behaviors you will like to control 30
    2. Calm down when you have impulsive thoughts 30
    3. Steer clear of triggers and find a healthy distraction 31
    4. Make consequences of defaulting vivid 31
    5. Make your plan time-bound 32
DAY 7: BE MORE RESPONSIBLE 33
    So why then should we be responsible? 33
    The easy way out! 34
    Way forward? 34
DAY 8: BOOST YOUR EFFICIENCY 37
DAY 9: DO SMART WORK AND MANAGE YOUR TIME 41
DAY 10: BE A MASTER AT SOMETHING 45
    1. Observe and learn 46

2. Start doing it 47
3. Train others 47
DAY 11: MANAGE YOUR PERSONAL FINANCE 49
DAY 12: IMPROVE YOUR MEMORY AND BOOST YOUR BRAIN POWER 53
DAY 13: YOU MUST LEARN HOW TO SAY NO 57
DAY 14: LEARNING TO FORGIVE 61
1. Think over the incident that made you angry 62
2. Shift your thoughts to the other person 63
3. Decide if it makes sense to you to tell the person that wronged you that you have forgiven him or her. 63
DAY 15: ACQUIRE COURAGE AND BE BOLDER 65
1. Stop playing too nice 65
2. Push yourself to talk more (when you have something to say) in groups 66
3. Think about the worst thing that can happen (but still go ahead) 66
4. Build momentum 67
DAY 16: MANAGE YOUR ANGER MORE EFFECTIVELY 69
DAY 17: IMPROVE YOUR SPIRITUAL LIFE 73
DAY 18: LEARNING TO CO-OPERATE BETTER WITH OTHERS 77
DAY 19: FIND INSPIRATION EVERY DAY 81
DAY 20: TRANSFORM YOURSELF TO A BETTER LISTENER 83
DAY 21: WORK ON YOUR COMPASSION 87
So how do you become more compassionate? 88
DAY 22: ACHIEVE EMOTIONAL INDEPENDENCE 91
DAY 23: GET ENOUGH SLEEP TO GET ON TOP OF YOUR DAY 95
DAY 24: DEALING WITH GRIEF 99
How to cope with grief. 100

DAY 25: TAKE GRATITUDE MORE SERIOUSLY 103
DAY 26: UNDERSTAND HOW TO MAKE BETTER AND MORE REWARDING DECISIONS 107
DAY 27: EAT HEALTHIER AND MAINTAIN A GOOD DIET 111
DAY 28: MANAGE STRESS MORE EFFECTIVELY 115
DAY 29: BE A BETTER LEADER 119
DAY 30: CELEBRATE YOUR VICTORIES TRANSFORMING YOURSELF 123
ABOUT THE AUTHOR 125

DAY 1:

POSITIVE AFFIRMATIONS TO SELF

Our actions as human beings are manifestations of our thoughts, some self-generated; others a projection of other people's perspective. But the crux of the matter is that we are what we think, just as the food we eat has numerous implications on our growth and development, so does our thoughts. That's why it is imperative that we guard our mind jealously and be careful of what kind of thoughts emanates from it.

But to be objective and look at things more logically, thoughts are just thoughts if it doesn't give rise to actions. But before thoughts get converted to actions, a lot of the time, words play a huge role.

Words acts as a conduit for the conversion of thoughts into action. This is why we also have to be very careful in choosing our words when dealing with ourselves and other people.

But a lot of us engage in negative mental chatter. We are always constantly flooding our brain with negative thoughts: thoughts filled with guilt about our past or current actions and anxiety about our future. We think about this so much that at a certain stage we start to convert these negative thoughts about ourselves to words especially when we are facing some little challenges in life.

Statements like these begin to overcome our true potential for success: "How can I pass this exam when I'm not that smart?"

"My boss can't consider me for a promotion" "I'm not good enough"

"If only I was tall enough"

" If only I had rich parents."

A lot of studies and real-life scenarios have gone to show that engaging in negative self-talk is a recipe for disaster especially in the area of self-esteem and self-confidence. Any seed of negativity sown today can grow to destroy a lot of positive values in your life.

In your path to self-development and transformation, the words you speak to yourself matters a great deal and that's why you should speak to yourself only things that benefit you and will contribute to your wellness. That's where positive affirmations to self comes in. The word 'affirmation' derives its meaning from the Latin word, *affirmare*, which means "to strengthen."

Affirmations help to strengthen your belief in the power of an action you intend to execute. Engaging in affirmations every day helps to wire your brain to believe the fact that nothing is truly impossible. Positive affirmations are proven methods of self-improvement because of its potential to "re-work" the brain and increase the level of "feel-good" hormones in our body. It will help you see things in different light, purifying your thought by stripping away all negative influence that can hinder the execution of the action you are planning to take.

By making positive, verbal affirmations daily about your dreams and ambition, you will start becoming empowered with the depth of assurance that your wish will very soon be transformed to reality. If you can change the way you think and the words you speak to yourself, you can change the world to come to your favor. It is normal to desire personal growth, financial independence, emotional, physical and spiritual development and engaging in positive self-talk can make you achieve that by putting in motion the necessary actions that can make that possible.

Identifying negative internal chatter

The first step to eliminating negative self-talk is to first know what it looks like. You must first of all get intimate with the thoughts that run through your mind and pick off the negative thoughts.

Awareness will help you pick out these negative chatter so you can deal with them decisively. If you have a long history of negative self-talk say for instance, your step-father repeatedly told you as a kid that "you are slow" or "you are never going to amount to anything", you might grow up believing this to be true. You will find that most times when you engage in deep introspection, you might believe this to be true, you might even think that your "slowness" is the reason you are in this current stage in life. You will find that the thoughts in your head will be filled with talk of "learning is so hard" or "Success is not for me."

If these are the kind of stories you tell yourself on a constant basis, then your actions are going to show signs of low self-esteem and self-confidence. You can't really soar in life if what you do is pull yourself down constantly.

Another trait of negative internal chatter is "I can't." When you tell yourself that you can't fulfill a dream or make a wish come true for yourself because you feel that you "don't have the courage, stature, height, body size" or "financial resources" or "intelligence" to achieve it, then you are creating a mental isolation for yourself.

You must remove "I can't" from your mental vocabulary and twist it to "Why can't I?"

Implanting Positive Affirmations

Your positive affirmations should be short, believable, and focused statements. By repeating it to yourself over and over every day, you are navigating territories into your subconscious and spreading wide open the possibility of new and useful thoughts. You must always ensure to read your affirmations aloud and with feelings. You shouldn't just read them, but must believe in them. You must complement this affirmation with emotion and the faith that you are not merely confessing them.

Here are 50 examples for you to engage in depending on whatever situation you find yourself in.

When feeling lonely

1. I am a very unique and beautiful creation in all of the universe
2. I acknowledge my own self-worth; my confidence is increasing
3. I enjoy my own company
4. Happiness is a choice. I base my happiness on my own accomplishments and the blessings I've been given
5. I am too exciting and gifted to wallow in self-pity
6. Today, I am radiating with energy and overflowing with joy
7. I love myself and need no one's validation
8. I radiate beauty, charm, and grace

When you are feeling terrified without any danger in sight

1. I am strong, nothing shall terrify me
2. I make the right choices every time
3. (If you're married) My marriage is becoming stronger, deeper, and more stable as each day passes
4. I trust myself to keep me safe

5. I am a powerhouse; I am indestructible
6. I draw from my inner strength and light
7. My strength to conquer my challenges is boundless; my potential to succeed is limitless

When it seems like you don't matter

1. I am smart and have a lot to offer the world
2. I matter and I possess what the world needs
3. Creative energy surges through me and leads me to new and brilliant ideas
4. I am a unique human in all the 7 billion on earth
5. I have been given endless talents which I begin to utilize today

When you are afraid

1. I trample upon fear and take prideful courageous steps
2. Wonderful things are happening to me
3. The outcome of this situation will be for my good
4. I am superior to bad thoughts and low actions

When you are angry

1. I let go of anger so I can find inner peace
2. I accept responsibility for my actions and move forward
3. I clean my anger with understanding and sound reasoning
4. I move past all the mistakes I've made as a result of my anger
5. I forgive those who have harmed me in my past and peacefully detach from them
6. A stream of compassion wipes away my anger and replaces it with love

When you feel like all hope is lost

1. I chose to find a hopeful and more optimistic way to look at this problem
2. I can't give up now, hope is on the way
3. (For business owners) My business is growing, expanding, and thriving
4. The situation may not look good now, but it will very soon
5. I am conquering my illness; I am defeating it steadily each day
6. I am courageous and I stand up for myself
7. My future is an ideal projection of what I envision now
8. My efforts are being supported by the universe; my dreams transform into reality before me

When you can't make up your mind about a decision

1. I trust my intuition and wisdom to make the best decision
2. I love my family even when they don't understand me completely
3. I am at peace with all that has happened, is happening, and will happen
4. I am a better person because of the past experience(s) that I've had.

When you are with friends

1. I choose friends who won't put me down
2. My friends are not judges over my life and what I do
3. My friends are still my friends even if we disagree from time to time
4. I am blessed with an incredible family and wonderful friends
5. Many people look up to me and recognize my worth; I am admired

In conclusion, replacing negative self-talk with a positive one won't happen within the twinkle of an eye. It will take some work on your own part and time for your mind to completely absorb this positive. If you are willing to commit to this process every day, the change will happen faster than you think.

DAY 2:

IMPROVE YOUR SELF-ESTEEM

In life, nothing is as important as the way you feel and think about yourself. But unfortunately, in the world that we live in today, low self-esteem is highly pervasive especially as most people today live their lives in eternal and unfair comparison with friends on social media, in school, at work etc. A high opinion of yourself, a sense of who you are and basically a love for yourself are very important in your mental and social development and more often than not are indicators of a successful life.

Having a low self-esteem typically means that you have negative ideas about your person in terms of self-worth and value and numerous reasons can account for this feeling. For example

- Unfair comparison of yourself to others
- Ignoring your accomplishments
- Being overly critical of yourself and dwelling on the negatives
- Negative self-talk
- Not accepting compliments given

Like any problem in life, the first step to solution is an understanding of the causation. But there are many underlying reasons responsible for a low self-esteem. Here are a few:

- Poverty and unemployment
- Poor grades in school

- Loneliness
- Bullying
- Neglect
- A feeling that you are odd

The list could actually be longer but these are just common ones. Sometimes, identifying the source of your low self-esteem may not be so straight-forward and it might be difficult to determine where and when it first started. Nonetheless, no matter the cause, there are actionable steps that you can take to nip the problem in the bud and bring your self-confidence to the level to which it belongs.

1. Silence your inner critic

There is nothing as good as being able to control your inner critic when it is processing discouraging thoughts. Wondering what an inner critic is? First of all, everyone has it. It is that voice in your head that whispers discouraging and destructive thoughts and becomes louder any time you hit an emotional bump or go through a rough patch in life. You will recognize it when it tells you that:

- You are fat and that's why you can't get a date
- Someone will take over your job because you do such a sloppy job
- You are the ugliest amongst your friends
- You can't get a job because of your college grades

But you have a choice in silencing this thought. You have a choice in deciding the statements that define you. There are ways to stomp these negative thoughts and replace them with more positive thoughts that can help you grow.

You must learn to say "STOP" when the inner critic is trying to taint your mind with the negatives and try to recalibrate your mind to focus on something more constructive like your achievements, your dreams, your dinner plans, your next football game, the movie you want to go see with friends, etc.

2. Don't compare your life to that of other people

Albert Einstein was known to have said, "If you judge a fish by its ability to climb a tree, it will live its life believing that it is no good." Everyone has their strength and weakness. Just as they have what makes them excel, the part they project in public and the part that people envy and want to associate with such as money, good looks, amiable personality, etc., they also have their insecurities, and it could be a bad parent, spouse, or child. They might even be in debts. So the point is don't measure your worth with others. It is just unfair to you.

3. Learn to handle mistakes and failures more positively

Everyone makes mistakes; your gardener, the guy at Target or Starbucks, President Obama, Ernest Hemmingway, you, me, everybody. So don't beat yourself up about it. If you leave your comfort zone to try to do something that is meaningful to you, expect that you may fall along the way—and that's alright—because it's your 'uncomfortable' zone. It's OK to stumble. It's alright to fall. But each time you do, be your own best friend. Don't beat yourself up, instead ask yourself how you would support your friends if they were in your shoes. This will help you become more constructive after the pain of a mistake or a failure starts to dissipate.

4. Do something different

When you try something new every once in a while, you are challenging yourself to do something you've never done before and consequently opening up your self-esteem for improvement. It is not about doing the new task in a way Steve Jobs (a perfectionist) would have wanted it. What matters is that you tried. You didn't just sit and do nothing. For that, you should appreciate yourself.

Therefore, go outside your comfort zone more often. Don't expect stellar results from the very start, just do something for the fun of it. Then later, continue doing it to improve your performance. If it feels too scary and uncomfortable at first, don't beat yourself up. It is supposed to feel that way.

What you should do is carefully and gently take smaller steps towards it, you will be surprised at how easy it will become.

5. Be kinder to others

There is a saying that, "people will forget what you give them, they will even more likely forget what you told them, but they won't forget how you made them feel." When you treat others kindly and think of yourself in a kinder way, people will start thinking of you kindly in the long run too. So be kind in your daily life. For example:

- Allow others to vent their anger while you listen
- Encourage someone when they are down
- Hold up the door to allow the next person in
- Allow someone in your lane when driving
- Help a senior shop for groceries

6. Spend more time with people who support you

No matter how hard you try to keep your self-esteem up, if the most important people in your life drag you down ever so constantly, then your efforts are going to end up futile. Therefore, make changes to what you receive. Spend less time with people who are nervous perfectionists, unkind and unsupportive of your life's dream and goals. But instead, spend more time with people who are more positive, uplifting, and human and have kinder ways of thinking about things especially when it involves you.

Also, try to sieve what you read, watch, and listen to. Don't spend unnecessary time on internet forums that don't add value to you. Stop reading a magazine, blog, website or TV show that makes you doubt and feel more negative about yourself. Instead read books and listen to podcasts that positively re-enforces a stronger belief in yourself and your abilities.

In conclusion, it is imperative to say this: the simple way to become consistent at something is to remember the most important reasons you are doing it. So today, you must never forget why you should stop comparing yourself with friends, spend more time around people that support you, and treat yourself and others kindly. They are the passageway to a destination of high self-esteem and confidence.

DAY 3:

BREAK A BAD HABIT

You know what bad habits are, more importantly, you know what your own bad habits are. Bad habits generally tend to put our lives in jeopardy, health-wise and socially. They subject our mental, physical, and social lives to unnecessary risk. What more? They waste your time and effort.

So what can you do about them?

The first step is understanding and conceding that habits which the people around you consider undesirable or puts your life at risk is bad and should therefore be changed. Concession will allow you look for the root cause of your bad habits; which is the wisest strategy when looking for a solution.

What's responsible for bad habits?

Majority of bad habits are caused by two things: stress and boredom. The need to engage in something to fill the void created by these two things is what birth bad habits. That's why people bite their nails or overspend on a shopping spree or drink every weekend or spend too much time on Facebook, Twitter, and Reddit, or play PlayStation and Xbox from sun up to sun down. People do all these to respond to boredom.

But, it doesn't always have to happen like that. You can engage in healthier ways to deal with stress and boredom which you can swap for your bad habits.

Of course, there is no denying that bad habits can be triggered by issues that transcend boredom and stress in depth. These issues might be tough life issues. But nonetheless, if you indeed want to change these bad habits, you can! If you recognize the root cause.

You replace a bad habit, you can't remove it

Believe it or not, the bad habits you are currently engaged in are providing you with benefits whether psychological like biting your nails or biological like smoking or drugs. Sometimes, it could even be emotional like staying in an abusive relationship. And in many cases bad habits just help people deal with navigate stress. For example, pulling your hair, tapping your foot, clenching your jaw, etc.

Because bad habits provide some comfort for you, that's exactly why you can't eliminate them but instead replace them with a good habit that provides you with the same benefit. Perhaps, you smoke when you are stressed or angry, the best way to prevent smoking when you are stressed or angry is to find a replacement habit not the general idea to "just quit smoking."

The best way to break a habit is to replace it with a healthier behavior that satisfies the same need that the bad habit is addressing.

So how do you that? How do you actually break a bad habit?

Select a replacement for your undesirable habit

You need to create a plan for how you will cope with the stress or boredom that your current bad habit is satisfying when you want to eliminate it. What should you do when you feel the urge to smoke? Will you go for breathing exercises? Will you go for a long walk avoiding routes where cigarettes can be found? What about when the red social media notification button flashes continuously on your screen? Would you engage in 30 minutes of serious work instead? Whatever your exit plan is, it should include a replacement strategy.

Reduce the triggers as much as you can

If drinking makes you smoke, then don't go to the bar. If you eat chocolate bars each time you set your eyes on them, then don't put them in the house. If the first thing you do is pick up your gaming console as soon as you enter the sitting room, then keep the console upstairs where it will be more difficult to reach. Get triggers off the way, that's the only way to make things easier.

Watch out for the urges, and delay for as long as possible.

You will get urges to engage in/return to your bad habits, that's for sure. These are dangerous if you just act on them without giving them a second thought. Do well to recognize them as soon they show up, and just watch them rise and fall, without acting. Pull back yourself, if you really want to act on the urge. Breathe out. Drink a cup of water. Call someone to help you out. Go for a long walk. Get out of the situation. The urge will go away, if you just stand your grounds.

Tell a friend or relative

It is normal to not want to tell people that you are breaking a habit, sometimes it could be because you don't want to feel embarrassed about your habits. Other times, it could be the fear of failure that's keeping you. But the truth is, there are lots of advantages in telling somebody or pairing up with someone who wants to quit too. Telling a friend will ensure that someone is monitoring you as you reach each milestone and they can help you avoid the major triggers while keeping your mind focused on the major goal. Also, pairing with somebody who wants to quit the same habit ensures that you both can hold yourself accountable and celebrate together when you reach a milestone. In conclusion, knowing that someone has a high expectation of you in your attempt to get better is a powerful motivator.

See yourself succeeding

Endeavour to see yourself eating healthy food, waking up early, or stopping masturbation. Whatever bad habit is bugging you, being able to visualize success is very key.

Ditch the people who make you engage in your old ways

The point is not to advise you to leave your old friends. The point is this: you can't be breaking a drinking addiction when you hang out with your drinking buddies at the bar downtown. You can't break a porn addiction by hanging out all the time with friends who talk about sex every passing moment. Therefore, you should surround yourself with people who are living the way you want to live instead of those who will be drawing you back into the habit you are trying to break.

Factor in Failure

Don't think everything is suddenly going to start falling into place the moment you practice what we've been discussing. Expect to hit a bump one or twice. You might make a mistake along the way and you might not. But whatever you do, understand that it's all part of the process, don't beat yourself up over a mistake, but get back on track as quickly as possible, that's the only way to make up for the set back.

In conclusion, you should track how, when, and often you engage in these habits, so you can replace them. Here are helpful questions you might need.

- When does your bad habit actually happen?
- How many times do you do it each day?

- Where are you?
- Who are you with?
- What triggers the behavior and causes it to start?

Get a piece of paper in your pocket and a pen. Each time your bad habit happens, mark it down on a plain sheet of paper and at the end of the day, see how everything tallies up. Understand that the goal isn't to judge yourself or make yourself feel guilty about doing something unhealthy or unproductive when you do this. Simply keeping track of these issues will make you more aware of the behavior and give you lots of ideas for putting an end it.

DAY 4:

FIND YOUR LIFE'S PURPOSE

At certain points in your life, you are bound to feel confused, directionless, unmotivated, and unsure of what you want and why that is. Don't beat yourself up because you are not alone. This is a struggle every adult goes through one way or the other in life. Questions like, "What am I passionate about?" or "What do I do with my life" are characteristic of this emotional situation. You are not alone on the path to finding yourself and providing your life with true and deep meaning.

A part of the problem is the idea of the term "life's purpose." The assumption that we are born on earth to fulfill a higher purpose and we must search the depth of the earth to find it. But this is the truth. Our existence on earth is time-bound. During that period, we will engage in things. Some of those things are important and they give us happiness and fulfillment as end results. Others are unimportant and may well leave us with feelings of boredom, loneliness, and dissatisfaction. So, when people ask, "What am I passionate about?" or "What should I do with my life?" the answer they are seeking is "What can I do with my time that I won't get tired of and is bound to give me joy, happiness, and satisfaction?" This obviously is a far better question to ask compared to "What is my life's purpose?" because the goals are clear. It is also manageable and can be easily visualized.

Out there, there are tons of stories, books, and materials on how to find "purpose" in life. But a lot of those books sound very abstract and offer often impracticable and vague solutions. Which is why today, we are going to discuss steps that are much more realistic, practicable and achievable in the path to finding what it is you truly want to do with your life. Now, these steps are not a do-this-do- that-solution. They are steps to help you discover yourself by yourself and for yourself.

1. Ask yourself, what kind of activities do I not get tired of?

Now, let's be truthful. Everything in life involves some level of sacrifice and cost. Life is not made up of peaks, there are many valleys involved. So it is imperative to ask yourself, what is it that I love so much I can sacrifice and tolerate a lot for. This is important because what determines our ability to follow through with something we care and are concerned about is our ability to handle the downsides and sail through the storm when the time comes. If you want to be an entrepreneur in the food business and can't handle dwindling customers, then don't even bother starting it. If you want to venture into freelance writing and take hundreds of rejections personally, then you don't have enough passion and may probably not be successful. If you want to be an engineer and cringe at the first sight of a mathematical equation, then don't bother. The same way you can't be a lawyer if you don't like reading texts. Can you stay up till 4am coding in PHP? Are you able to still stand on stage even as people booed you off stage the last time you tried standup comedy? If you are not motivated enough to go through the storm for an endeavor, then you are probably not going to be successful at it. Drop it before you realize 5 or 10 years down the line that you've wasted your time.

2. Ask yourself, what is it I really want to do but I'm scared of?

A lot of the time, before you get very good at an activity, you must have tried your hands on other things and realized that they just aren't for you because why? You are terrible at those things. This means that before you can come to the conclusion that you are terrible at something, you must have tried it, got embarrassed by it often repeatedly, and acknowledge to yourself that you suck at it.

But this is where the problem of most people come from, they don't even try things before concluding that it isn't for them. They don't want to try something because it might embarrass them, or they don't know what their parents will say or think or they don't know how people will respond? But the question is, how would you know if you never tried? How would you know that you have the talent of acting if you have never really acted in front of people? The truth is if you keep avoiding something that has a decent level of risk involved, then you will never do something that feels important or magical!

As you are reading this, I'm sure there is something you've been fantasizing about doing but never really got to do because you've been justifying not doing it with "valid" reasons.

Sure, if the reason you can start a clothing line now is because your kids are still young and you need to nurture them to a certain age where they are a bit independent, then OK, but if it is, "My dad will not support me" or "it will be embarrassing to my church and friends," then that's a lazy excuse.

Why? Because you are not scared that your dad will not support you, you are only scared of living your fantasy.

Therefore, to find that path that will lead you to happiness, embrace risk and embarrassment because great things don't just happen to people. People make them happen. So get scared, feel foolish & act today because you will be smarter & more courageous tomorrow.

3. Ask yourself, how can I help people?

Let's assume you are not passionate about anything other than watching movies on replay while eating any unhealthy food, there is something else you can do. And that's contributing your own small quota in making the world a better place to live. There are lots of stuff you can do. Volunteer for a non-profit group, help seniors and physically-challenged people find their way, start a campaign against domestic abuse, etc. The list is endless.

Sometimes, we are much able to find a meaning for our lives when we discover that there are other people who are in need of our strength, love, courage, kind words and gestures and by reaching out to them, we find this meaning. We find values that transcend our own pleasure and satisfaction and this gives us happiness and contentment. Therefore, find a problem that the world needs solution to and start making a difference.

Finding a purpose for one's life actually boils down to the search for something that is greater than one's self, getting off the couch to act on it, while listening to one's inner voice and shunning external noise.

DAY 5:

LEARN TO HANDLE REJECTION NICELY

We know how the pain of rejection feels, whether you were excluded from a social gathering, passed up for a promotion, let out of a news scoop, sent a job reject mail, denied a loan request or denied admission from your dream institution. It could get really painful and everyone has a story or two to share about their personal experiences. Regardless of what your story is, here are a few tactics to putting a stop to the negative feelings rejection might be causing you.

1. **Acknowledge rejection**

   Instead of suppressing, ignoring or even denying the way rejection is making you feel, admit it. It is OK to be embarrassed, sad, disappointed or discouraged. There is no need to "act like a man" and bottle up your feelings. If it makes you cry, shed a tear, let the feeling out, and face them head-on. You might want to stay off social media for that period to avoid the temptation of updating your status or tweeting about it. The internet doesn't forget whatever you post and upload. Talk to someone like a friend or relative about the rejection, that way you will feel 'emotionally light' and that will make it easy for you to move forward. But avoid complaining unnecessarily, otherwise, you are going to end up feeling depressed.

2. Treat yourself with compassion

Instead of saying to yourself, "Idiot, how can you do that?" Treat yourself with compassion and speak positively to yourself. Speak kindly and affirmatively. Even if you were dumped by your long- term love or recently fired, overthinking and stressing about it won't solve a thing.

3. Don't take rejection personally

Understand that being rejected has nothing to do with who your person is. It is part of life and doesn't mean you should stop aiming high. That the publisher rejected your work or the girl rejected your proposal of a relationship doesn't mean something is wrong with you. They don't know you well enough so they can't judge you or write you off. For example, you asking a girl or a guy out and they saying "no" doesn't mean you are worthless. It simply means they are not interested in the request and that could be for numerous reasons; they are in a relationship, they aren't ready to date, etc.

4. Engage yourself in something else

When you are done acknowledging rejection, don't immediately get back to that activity or person that's the source of the rejection. Perhaps, you applied for a job and the company sent you a reject mail stating that they can't move forward with your application, you don't need to immediately whip out your pen and start scribbling another job application. Instead, go to the movies with a friend, visit a new place, and stay off your email for a day or two. This will allow you douse that feeling of rejection and make you conduct a personal evaluation so that you can feel refreshed and have a clear head when making your next application.

5. See rejection as a challenge

Many courageous people see rejection as a challenge and for some it serves as a proof that they are alive and living life to its peak. And to be candid, if you have never been rejected before in your plan to achieve something then you have not been challenging yourself and you may be living too far inside your comfort zone. Being turned down every once in a while could be proof that you are pushing yourself to the limit. When you get rejected for a project, passed up for a job, or turned down by a friend, you'll know at least that you are challenging yourself.

6. Learn from it

Now, that it has been said that rejection is normal. It should further be repeated that you should use every opportunity to learn from rejection. Rather than sit down and think about why it happened to you, think instead about why it happened and what lesson you can learn from it. Think about it in the areas you are found wanting by asking for feedback. Use rejection as an opportunity to step forward.

7. Don't let rejection affect your future

Understand that every situation is unique and every rejection is different. You must learn to accept that things might not work the way you want them to all the time and that's OK. The fact that one thing didn't work doesn't mean you are a failure or that everything else you engage in will not work out. If one guy says no to a date, it doesn't mean that every guy would and it doesn't mean also that you shouldn't ask other guys you find interesting to a date because one turned you down earlier.

Every instance is different. If you always believe that you will be rejected, then you won't be successful. Keep moving forward, don't dwell on past rejections.

You can't let rejection grind all the good activities and feelings in your life to a halt because truthfully you are going to have lots of instances of rejection in your life (just like everyone). By moving on with your life and engaging in other things, you aren't letting rejection get the better of you.

DAY 6:

UNDERSTAND AND MANAGE SELF-CONTROL

A lot of factors contribute to our inability to control ourselves in lots of situations. And no, it is not because we are humans and weakness is part of our fundamentals! The chief reason is because indulgence is so much a better alternative.

Think about this for example, if what you desire is to eat a healthy meal, your best bet then will be a meal you cook yourself; a meal where you have the control over the choice of ingredients and nutrients you want to consume.

But, this requires a lot of work. It requires going to shop for the ingredients or order them over the Internet. It will require processing: cutting, dicing, washing, etc. And, also require time and patience for all the ingredients to transform into one fine meal. But your body cannot handle all that waiting time and effort, so it chooses to offer your brain a 'smarter' alternative—a takeout. A fatty takeout where you have no control over how it is prepared. Your brain accepts the offer because it seems like the satisfaction offered by a takeout is the same as that offered by cooking. It doesn't look at the long term effect of your indulgence in fatty food. Why? Because it is so easy to ignore when you are in that zone.

As humans, we can be terrible at predicting what the future will look like, we tend to indulge in what makes us feel good at the moment because the result of that can be easily seen as it is immediate. If you are not the type who enjoys fixing your own meal, then making yourself spend so much time, effort and resources to fix a meal of spaghetti in pasta sauce will be a lot harder than just ordering pizza as you watch an old episode of your favorite show on your big plasma TV.

Do you see where the problem lies? Self-control is the ability to stop yourself from making a bad decision (often with long-term consequences) based on immediate desire or gratification and motivating yourself to make better choice. No one said it will be easy. If it was, then there won't be a need for this piece and many other wisdoms you will find in all this theme in bookshops and over the internet!

But how should you go about it?

1. Make a list of behaviors you will like to control

The first step to working on your self-control is identifying the key behaviors you will like to change about yourself. Perhaps someone told you that you talk too much. Or you noticed yourself that you watch too much TV or can't stop yourself from thinking about sweet foods or fizzy drinks. Write all these down. Next, sit down and identify what triggers these behaviors. By recognizing what triggers these behaviors and makes you act impulsively, you'll be able to teach yourself how to delay the time between your thoughts and your actions.

2. Calm down when you have impulsive thoughts

Creating a time gap before your thoughts and actions help you evaluate your decisions more objectively and rationally. Perhaps, if you want to control yourself in the area of overspending, then decide that before you purchase anything, anything at all, you will give it 24 hours to actually think it through. You can write down the item you intend to purchase in a notebook so you won't forget. Then, after 24 hours, come back to check your list to see if you really need the item. Five out of ten times, you will change your mind because by the time you come back after 24 hours, the impulsive feeling would have gone.

3. Steer clear of triggers and find a healthy distraction

You will find it harder to quit drinking beer if when coming home from work, you take the route where there are lots of bars and night clubs. It certainly won't help. Instead, find an alternative route. Recognize what triggers the habits you are trying to control and distract yourself with something healthier. Perhaps you want to reduce how many times you masturbate a week or even want to stop altogether, a very good way to provide yourself with distraction is to always be around people who don't.

Since masturbation is facilitated by loneliness and triggered by porn materials, it only makes sense that you throw away your porn stash and avoid being alone all the time, especially when you are close to a pornographic or sexually-suggestive material.

4. Make consequences of defaulting vivid

If every time you walk into your closet, you see a very big, bloody, nauseous and disturbing image of the lungs of someone who died from cancer caused by cigarette smoking, what do you think it will do to you? Will it make you want to continue smoking? If you want to control yourself, you must learn to make the consequences of the action you are trying to stop very vivid. Fear is a good motivator when it comes to self-control. If you are allergic to peanuts, you will never eat peanut, no matter how much everybody is eating it because you know that the consequences are quite fatal. In order to use fear as a self-control tool, you must make the consequences of not controlling a behavior immediate and fatal. How you choose to do this is your personal choice. But as a suggestion, what you can do is spend time with people who represent the consequence and the result of the action you are trying to curb and think about them the next time you feel the urge to indulge in that habit.

5. Make your plan time-bound

Try doing it for a week for a start. If you spend 8 hours watching TV every day, try cutting it to five every day for an entire week. Granted, a week is not going to be enough time to get rid of any habit, but it sure can give you the confidence that you can actually control yourself. If you can try to stretch it to a month, which is enough time to get rid of a habit anyway, then you can actually control yourself. But understanding that you don't have to actually stop can make a big difference in giving yourself the conviction that you can actually conquer your impulse and can control yourself.

Learning to control yourself is not an easy task for the toughest of men and women but you'll get better with practice and if you are able to follow these strategies, it is only going to be a matter of time before you get rid of those nasty habits!

DAY 7:

BE MORE RESPONSIBLE

I'm sure you are not just reading this for the first time. "Be more responsible," "Take up more responsibility" And all other psychobabble about responsibility that you've heard since you were a kid. Many times in our lives, we've been admonished to be responsible, but no one ever told us why. Of course, without the necessary explanation for the action to take place, the message will fail to get delivered.

So why then should we be responsible?

To be candid, there really isn't any good alternative to being responsible. When we give up responsibility we become like a rudderless boat swayed left and right by the ocean waves, directionless and on a crash course. We lose control of everything when we lose control of ourselves and the things that matter to us. We head for doom because others will not resist the opportunity to take this control from us and use it for their selfish benefits and/or cause us harm and injury. So commonsense and logics wise, it only makes sense that we become responsible for our actions since we are going to be held accountable by it and because it is a major determinant of the events that are shaping our present and is going to shape our future.

The easy way out!

Of course, most people understand the forgoing. But executing responsible actions is what most people find difficult. The difficulty is that it feels way easier to allow someone else to make the important decision or do the grunt work for us while we come in and enjoy the success. But sadly, life doesn't work that way. We can allow people to have authority over us but we can't make them responsible for our actions and our happiness. These are forever our own responsibilities.

Way forward?

The good news is that there's a solution and the first step in that solution is to first acknowledge that life and things generally don't just happen to you; most times you have the ability to decide what happens and doesn't happen to you. You have a choice. You have the ability to choose. You have the ability to be responsible for your life. Of course, this is very easy to say than do. Accepting the fact that we have the choice to take responsibility for our actions, may often bring with it a wave of guilt about our actions (or inactions) in the past. But for others who have, through their actions or inactions, gone through lots of trauma, it is easier to go on believing that the events that happened in the past and its attendant consequence(s) happened because they didn't have any option, no control and so no responsibility.

But this way of thinking is just a convenient lie we tell ourselves to absolve ourselves of guilt. A better alternative to thinking about past errors or mistake is to accept them as what they are— mistakes. No one was born with the ability to make perfect decisions, we all learn from experiences as we grow older in age and it doesn't matter when or how long it takes to learn how to be responsible. Everyone learns at their own rate and there is no yardstick for measuring the duration.

There are other ways for you to begin to learn about choices and responsibilities.

One of them is, that whenever you are faced with a problem, whether emotional or practicable, take a breather, and refocus your mind clearly and objectively on the situation in front of you, reminding yourself that you are responsible. Ask yourself how you can tackle the problem. Remember the saying, "There are many ways to kill a rat…" For most problems in life, there are usually more than one single way to solve them. Only that they all might not just be the palatable, but at least there is a solution. Understand that there are always options and deciding to give up your own choices isn't always the best course of action to take.

Secondly, you might need to upgrade your skills in order to take action. You will find assertiveness a very useful strategy in your plan to take control of your life. It is available and easily accessible to as many people that need it.

Also, stop letting people take actions and solve problems for you. There are basically two reasons for this. First of all, in most cases, people can't. At least, not every time. The people that you surround yourself with, might be able to solve a particular terrible situation for you but you have to make sure that such a problem does not arise again. You must do away with dependence and take some time to learn the skills that you need to solve your own problems. Doing this will enable you to get over the fear that you can't do without people. Remember—you are a very responsible person. You can solve your own problems. Don't ever forget that.

Learn to accept and acknowledge feedbacks too. It is part of being responsible. Being open to criticism and acknowledging when someone has given you a feedback that can help you grow and improve your life as a person. If you want to be better at work, it makes sense to listen to your colleagues and superiors when they mention to you about areas that you need to focus on. If your friends tell you about a flaw you need to work on, don't just brush it off because you think that since they are your peers, they can't tell you what areas of your life you should improve on.

Lastly, take out the time to learn and implement a strategy to help yourself emotionally or psychologically if you are still finding things difficult. There are many techniques available and you can find them in other books or online articles. You don't need to be a therapist to pick out one that works but you can talk to one if you feel the need to.

DAY 8:

BOOST YOUR EFFICIENCY

Whether you are in the U.S.A, Scotland, Madagascar, Australia or Nigeria, you are going to have 24 hours to yourself. Sure, the time zones are different. You might just be waking up to start your day in Texas while your colleague doing field research at Tanzania is just wrapping the day's activities up and preparing to retire to bed. You will both have the same 24 hours to yourself. Now, what we do between those hours is what makes us successful or unsuccessful. So while you will want the sun to just extend its setting time by just a few hours (which won't happen by the way), here are strategies you can use to maximize your work habits and productivity.

Don't multitask. Of course, you've read it somewhere that the ability to multitask is a desired trait but that isn't true. And this is the truth: many times we fool ourselves into thinking we can handle many activities simultaneously but we just can't. Multitasking leads to distraction and inefficiencies in the execution of tasks which will in the end require more time and energy to fix. Only A very few people in the world can solidly focus and handle more than one task at a time; especially tasks that extremely requires focus.

Because of the illusion that being able to do 3 or 4 tasks at the same time is good, many of us believe that we can get more done within a short period of time when in reality we are accomplishing less and the quality of our work is poor.

Also, learn to delegate task to others. You won't be able to do everything by yourself. In fact, no machine ever built can. Don't believe all the stories you hear about successful people staying up late 3am every day to accomplish tasks. It is a sign of inefficiency. If you are efficient, you will know the kind of task that you shouldn't stay up late at night doing, you will know what tasks to delegate to a friend, your kid, your partner, a co-worker or another teammate. You will know that only the most important of tasks that others can't do or can't do super-efficiently should be handled by you. When you understand how to break down a task and empower other people to contribute their efforts, you can select only the task that is most suited for you and work your way through them without distraction.

Learn to plan projects by breaking down tasks into smaller bits. You waste a lot of effort when you can't create for yourself a clear plan to success. Impatience is the enemy of efficiency. To be able to do efficient work, you must be able to split giant tasks into smaller and easily achievable tasks in order to achieve consistent success. Planning may take long but being able to visualize the end goal and foreseeing the challenges, processes, and responsibilities well-ahead, will enable you have a clear knowledge of where you are headed and how to get there. And what's more, it's been found that the more time you spend planning, the less time you'll need to get the task done.

Put Parkinson's Law into use. "If you wait until the last minute, it only takes a minute to do."— Cyril Northcote Parkinson. You've seen this law work every time you struggle for a month, trying to get a project done before its deadline and all of a sudden, you are able to finish it in a week. Or when your apartment is in a mess for weeks and all of a sudden the condo becomes spotless and shiny within a few hours of the new girlfriend's visit. The law makes a case for efficiency through the imposition of shorter deadlines for a task or rescheduling an earlier meeting. Nevertheless, find a good enough deadline to do a work that is good but doesn't give you the opportunity to waste any more time than required.

You should also try to give everything a proper place. Really efficient people find a place to keep small but important items such as keys, pens, and clothing accessories which can be a source of distraction and frustration when they are missing. You can really be efficient when you are organized. Create a place for the storage of items you need very frequently. Organize your clothes, papers, and electronics in such a way that you can easily get access to it. It may take a few minutes to rearrange your place or workstation but the time you will save in future from searching for what's important cannot be compared to what you are going to expend now.

Take rest. Again, when people say they are workaholics and can work for 21 out of 24 hours, don't take their word for it. No one was born to work all day without rest. Even machines take scheduled breaks at least for maintenance. As you may well know, tired and overworked people don't perform really well. Don't sacrifice your resting period thinking that it makes you more efficient. The truth is that it doesn't. Efficient people make sure that they take scheduled rests, so they can perform better.

Learn to communicate more appropriately. Poor communication can often be a huge time-waster. A fast email containing bad or incorrect instructions on a project often brings with it more unnecessary hours. To be more efficient, learn to share your thoughts in clear, unambiguous ways. Send mails using the exact language and tone necessary to get the intended effect. It might take a little more time to achieve but in the future, it will save you more of the stress and time of revisiting what has been thought buried.

In conclusion, effect a work-rest ratio of 52:17. Where's this from? Desk Time App monitored the usage of computers by employees found out that the most productive 10 percent focused and worked hard for 52 minutes and then took a break for the next 17. This means that strategic breaks yield efficient work and you should therefore try to implement the '52:17 Principle.'

DAY 9:

DO SMART WORK AND MANAGE YOUR TIME

Yesterday, we talked about the fact that no single human has more time in a day than the rest of us. A quote by H. Jackson Brown Jr. seems to buttress that.

"Don't say you don't have enough time. You have exactly the same number of hours per day that were given to Helen Keller, Pasteur, Michael Angelo, Mother Teresa, Leonardo da Vinci, Thomas Jefferson, and Albert Einstein."

And this is exactly what makes time management a very important principle.

The society we live in today tends to make us want to get hyper-busy especially in this age of social media as everything is always screaming for attention—phone alarms, social media notifications, task managers, calls, SMSs, etc. The list is endless. Some of us, in a bid to be productive, try to engage and manage these numerous tasks by switching from one to another. We want to stay busy, but in the end all we do is waste time by engaging in mindless productivity. But task and time management isn't about squeezing as many tasks as possible into your day. It is about simplifying your work, doing things faster and giving you enough time to play, rest and spend time with the people that care about you.

See, there is a lot of time to do all the things you want in a day if you are able to prioritize and rearrange the things in your life to make enough room.

Here are a few suggestions on how you can achieve that.

Tackle the most important tasks of the day first. This seems to be the most important rule in time management. Every day, before you delve into work, look at the most important tasks to complete and tackle them first. Your most important task could be the task which poses the biggest risk if left unexecuted. Immediately you are able to achieve that task, then your day is almost close to being successful. You can then move on to other tasks on your list. It's okay even if you are not able to complete all other minor tasks in as much as you are able to do the task with the highest importance.

Focus on the task at hand. Whenever you are involved in any task, resist the temptation to get involved in any other task. Keep your phone away or put it on silent. Look for a very quiet place to work or listen to good music as you get to work. Get your focus on one task, nothing else should be on your mind. Focus on this one task, immerse yourself in it. Nothing else should be on your mind so you don't end up wasting good time as you become engrossed in other tasks.

Meanwhile, group related tasks together. Perhaps, over the weekend, you want to write a proposal for your business, write an article for your blog, finish a coding assignment, complete the literature review section of your dissertation, and try out a food recipe you saw online. Instead of doing this task in the order that they have been listed, it makes sense that you group the similar tasks together. For example, any activity that involves writing should be completed together; dissertation, blog, and proposal tasks should be done together, leaving only programming and food recipe tasks. The reason for this is because different tasks demand different types of thinking, so it only makes sense that you allow your mind to continue to flow in similar zones rather than switching unnecessarily to something that's going to require you to re-focus your mind.

When you have a waiting period between tasks, do something important with that time. Perhaps, you are at the hospital to see the dentist for treatment but you are told to wait in the reception area because the dentist is a bit busy with another patient. Instead of wasting the time sitting and getting upset about the dentist taking forever to attend to you, you can bring out your phone and respond to the emails and other notifications that are popping up on your phone. You can also use the opportunity to attend to your to-do list or read a magazine or novel.

Be mindful of the time you spend watching TV, playing games, or browsing the internet. These things are arguably the biggest productivity drains as a lot of time is spent surfing the internet doing things that extends your fun time without taking into consideration the number of useful hours that's been lost to guilty pleasures.

You must learn to say no. Making lots of time commitments can make us learn how to manage different engagements and our time. However, we should not allow it go too far. You should learn how to turn down engagements that will not allow you to focus on the important tasks. As an advice, you should only accept engagements that you have the time to see through and the passion to see successful.

Take adequate rest. Sleeping 6-8 hours every day doesn't mean you are lazy. In fact, your body needs it to function optimally. If you don't get enough rest, your body will find a way to make you suffer for it through pain, lack of focus, muscular weakness and tiredness. Therefore, learn to listen to your body and make it have the rest it desires.

Attach a time limit to a task. Instead of just approaching a task with the mindset that you are not going to leave it until you are done with it, it helps to actually set a time limit to the execution of a task. You can for example, say "I'm going to spend 2 hours writing 2000 words for my blog." This time constraint will help you become more focused and efficient even if at the expiration of the two hours, you will still need to add a few more minutes to meet the 2000 words target.

In conclusion, you should never get so caught up in being busy that you forget to enjoy what you are doing. Even if your focus is to work smarter and manage your time, still take the time to enjoy whatever it is that you are doing because that matters a lot as well.

DAY 10:

BE A MASTER AT SOMETHING

The world we live in today, is skills-driven. A skillful workforce is what makes a business establishment thrive and reach for the zenith in the niche area such business is operating. Even on a personal level, there is a great need to acquire skills for personal growth and development of the self. Example of such skill may include money management, painting, interior decoration, public speaking, writing or cooking, just to name a few.

But attaining mastery at a particular skill or area of human endeavor is not something that one simply dreams to aspire to. It is the result of a combination of factors such as drive or passion, etc. and a greater portion of directed practice and opportunity.

Lots of books have been written on mastery, popular bestsellers like Malcolm Gladwell's Outliers explains using stats and facts that people like Beethoven and Bill Gates who are extremely good and successful at a particular field excel not because they are born with the brain of a genius but because they practiced for over 10,000 hours; the time which another book, Mastery (by Robert Greene), agrees with is the minimum hours required for someone to be a master at a particular skill.

If you pore through many literature and internet articles enough, you will find many strategies that work but to save you all that stress, here is a simple process that will make you a master if you are ready to take up the challenge and become a master at what you do.

There is a disclaimer however before we start. Understand that the fact that the process is said to be simple doesn't mean it is very easy or fast. No. It only means that it is the most straightforward approach to being a master at the skill of choice.

Here are the following three steps:

1. Observe and learn

To be great at something, you need a great teacher and it doesn't matter whether it is in the classroom or in a business environment. You need someone who has gone ahead of you to show you how it is done first. A quote attributed to Pablo Picasso reads, "learn the rules like a pro, so you can break them like an artist." You must keep all your learning senses (vision, smell, sound, speech and feelings) alert during this stage. Make sure to ask questions and ensure that you constantly in tune with what you are trying to master.

Perhaps you are trying to learn a new language, you need someone to teach you the basics of the language. For example, structure, sentence construction, tenses, building blocks of words, letters and sounds before you try to speak such a language. The same reason some fields like engineering and building construction require the completion of an internship program before the award of a degree or certificate. If you must really learn a skill, find the best teacher, go to the best school, download the best materials, visit the best forums, and contact the best in the field. You need a great teacher to show you the way.

Business leaders, doctors and other professionals need to first intern. If you want to learn how to do it, you will need to find a great teacher to show you.

2. Start doing it

The second best way to excel at learning a skill is to practice what you have learnt. Like the saying goes, "Use it or lose it." With the tool you need and a constant exposure to the skill you desire to acquire, the next step is to start practicing right away with your teacher or guide keeping a good eye on you, monitoring you and providing you with appropriate feedback.

Perhaps you are a builder, create your first framework for inspection. If you are a leader, take charge and oversee a project. This stage is very important. Your practice must be focused and directed at a particular thing. If your aim is to learn a language, focus on Spanish and learn that first. Don't learn Icelandic and Spanish together, because even though your aim is to learn a language, not narrowing down and spreading yourself too thin can make you lose sight of both.

Also, expect to fail at your first or second attempt. It is all part of self-development. If you don't mispronounce a word, you can't learn the right way to pronounce it. Now failure doesn't mean defeat until you decide not to try. Failure is very critical in mastery. Therefore, you must be courageous because along the way, you will fall and fail, and you will only stand upright if you are willing to.

Mastery of a skill can only come from failing, taking risk and being willing to be taught as you continue to try and learn how to do it better, faster and simpler. Until that day when you become a master.

3. Train others

This is the stage where many close to mastery at their chosen skill tripped and fell behind. The final strategy to achieving mastery in any area is to teach it to others. Albert Einstein once said, "If you cannot teach it to a twelve-year old, then you don't fully understand it." If you are truly a master at something, then you should be able to cement your mastery by teaching others too. If you ever want to test your understanding of a subject, try teaching someone else. Teaching others enables you to build upon other skills such as, adaptability, patience and the ability to see problems and solutions through a new lens because your students are bound to ask you questions you may have no answer to at first.

In conclusion, don't keep telling yourself that you do not have any time or opportunity to learn a new skill. Go ahead and practice all we've discussed.

DAY 11:

MANAGE YOUR PERSONAL FINANCE

The area of personal finance is one of the most important areas of self-development that needs to be heavily and continuously discussed. As Robert Kiyosaki, author of Rich Dad, Poor Dad and many others have rightly posited, the school system does not equip us with enough skills to be successful in life—and of the most important of such skills, is money management. Other skills such as, critical thinking and creativity followed closely.

As children, most of us are advised to go to school, get good grades, get good jobs and everything will be alright. But as adults, our reality has changed. The global financial crisis that forced industry giants like Lehman Brothers out of business in 2008 has made a lot of things much clearer to us. We now understand that going to school, getting a doctorate and even saving money in the bank doesn't always translate to a successful financial life.

Financial education is important to all and that's why in the following paragraphs, we'll be discussing a few tips on how you can manage your personal finance.

The best thing you can do for yourself when managing your personal finance is to create a budget. A budget, is a great way to track your income and spending. By creating a budget, you are less likely to be involved in bad debts. You are also more likely to have a good credit rating and be accepted for a mortgage or loan. Tracking your income and expenditure will also help you watch out for areas where you can make your savings and put you in a great position to save up for a holiday, a new car, etc. To create a good budget, you will need a knowledge of the amount you spend on household bills, living costs, financial products like insurance, travel costs, leisure and entertainment costs.

Secondly, you must learn to save. Some people find it hard to get motivated about saving, the truth is that it could really be hard when you have to put all the things you want to buy on hold just so you could save some money for the future. But it is much easier if you'll just set a goal. You must have some emergency savings— some amount of money to fall back on if you have an emergency, say you are involved in an accident and might be immobile for a while. In planning your emergency savings, try to get three months' worth of expenses in an easy access account. It's okay if you can't save it immediately, but make this your target.

Once you are able to do this, then you can move on to other savings goal that will allow you buy a car without taking a car loan or have some money while on maternity or paternity leave.

Alternatively, as your savings start to grow, you should think about investing it. You can consider a pension plan or make other sound investment decisions based on your goals and time frames.

Thirdly, try your best to stay off debts. Avoid high interest credit cards and do well to resist the urge to buy on impulse. Pay off all debts the moment you have the money to. If you have loans or owe money on credit cards, it usually makes sense to pay off the debt that charges the highest rate of interest first. Also, learn to delay gratification. If you are the type that shops to overcome boredom, find other things that might interest you. Try not to buy things when you're hungry, angry, lonely, or tired because you're at your weakest state mentally.

Consider passive income. Saving is a good habit to adopt. Budgeting is also a good money management practice but the most important of all personal finance strategies is to increase your streams of income. You can do this by getting involved in side businesses. A good area is the real estate business. But ultimately, you should do enough research to find out which area you are interested in based on passion and profitability. Profitability being the major factor.

In conclusion, get the 'stakeholders' in your life involved in whatever financial plan you are making. If you are cutting costs that you consider unnecessary as a married person, it is very important that you notify your significant other as what you consider unnecessary might be important to him or her. Talk to your kids, parents and whomever is going to be impacted by your plan so you don't start having issues at execution.

DAY 12:

IMPROVE YOUR MEMORY AND BOOST YOUR BRAIN POWER

You may have heard a lot of people say, "You can't teach an old dog a new trick," but they are incorrect as far as neuroscientists are concerned. Your brain has a jaw-dropping ability to adapt and morph to accommodate new learning curves even at old age. The ability to do this is what scientists call 'Neuroplasticity.' Research has shown that with the right stimulation, your brain can form new neural pathways, change existing connections, and adapt to accommodate many changes.

Therefore, don't think that you are too old to learn anything or improve your memory. It doesn't matter whether you are a mom with kids and need to sit for an examination or a professional looking for ways to stay mentally sharp and a senior searching for ways to avoid memory loss, there are lots of ways to spike up your mental alertness and better yourself. You can tap into the natural power of your brain's ability to reshape itself and enhance its potential to learn new information whilst improving your memory.

How can you do this?

First of all, engage in a brain workout.

By the time you become an adult, your brain would have developed millions of neural pathways that can help you recall and process information very quickly, solve problems that are familiar, and complete tasks with the smallest of mental efforts. But if you continue to use these old pathways, your brain will not develop. Therefore, you should periodically stimulate your brain. Because memory is like an acquired skill, if you don't use it, you will lose it. The more you stimulate and exercise your brain, the better it gets at acquiring information and processing it. Therefore, engage in an activity that will challenge your brain and help it to create new neural pathways. A good brain stimulation exercise should tick the following:

1. Something new: You must know that regardless of the intellectual demands of an activity, if it is something you are already good at, then you are not tasking your brain. You are not helping it. You must engage in an activity that will get your brain out of its comfort zone. Perhaps, you've always watched people play Scrabble, Chess, or a computer game like Gears of War and never tried playing it yourself before, you will be doing your brain, more good if you just give it a trial for once.

2. Something challenging: A very good brain-improving activity will demand your attention. It must be something that requires mental effort. Perhaps you are learning how to play the keyboard or a bass guitar, playing an already memorized piece will not make you improve. You will only improve by playing pieces that you are not familiar with.

3. Something you can eventually build on: You must look for an activity that has a learning vertical. Each stage must lead to a tougher stage so you can keep getting better. When you are reading for your exam and discovered that you are getting a lot of high scores in the practice questions in that book, then you should know it is time to check out a better textbook or the Internet for harder questions to be sure that you understand the concepts being taught.

4. Something rewarding: A rewarding activity challenges and motivates your brain to want to perform better. The higher your interest and performance in an activity, the better you are likely to continue and become successful at it. Therefore, you should select an activity that you will find challenging, enjoyable, and motivating.

    Think about an activity you've always wanted to engage in, like playing the keyboard, making sculptures or paintings, playing chess or backgammon, dancing the tango, playing tennis or soccer. These are nice examples of activities that can keep you challenged and keep your brain active.

Secondly, endeavor to exercise regularly. Physical exercise allows the flow of oxygen into your brain and helps reduce the risk of disorders that can lead to memory loss, such as diabetes and heart- related diseases. Exercising also helps in boosting growth factors and improving new neural pathways. In selecting an exercise, choose one that keeps your blood pumping. You should also consider others that require hand-eye coordination or complex motor skills.

Sleep is highly important if you want to give your brain a massive boost in retaining memory. Many people think that sacrificing sleep for work makes them efficient, but this isn't so. The truth of the matter is, that to avoid what is called sleep deprivation, your brain needs at least 7 to 9 hours of good sleep. If you don't give it that, you will be compromising your memory, creativity, problem-solving abilities, and critical thinking skills.

To ensure that you sleep well to boost your brain, you must sleep on a regular schedule, avoid all screens such as mobile phones, TVs, PCs at least an hour before you go to bed. Finally, you must reduce the caffeine content of your diet. Caffeine is widely known as a causative agent for sleep deprivation.

To round up today's lesson, you must learn to pay attention to things. You can't learn something if you don't pay attention to it. You must also endeavor to make connections between what you already know and what you are just learning. Whenever you learn something, always make sure to practice it, that way, you won't lose what you've learnt. And lastly, if you are ever going to involve yourself in the memorization of a complex material, use mnemonics. Don't know what mnemonics are? They are the cues that help us remember something. For example, in high school mathematics, you were taught BODMAS (Bracket Of Division Multiplication Addition & Subtraction) or PEMDAS (Please Excuse My Dear Aunty Sally) to help you remember the correct order of solving an algebraic expression.

DAY 13:

YOU MUST LEARN HOW TO SAY NO

You must have heard the saying, "Good fences make good neighbors." This is not about being antisocial but about the ability to set firm boundaries. By setting boundaries, we have the liberty to behave in ways that satisfy our interests with fewer distractions and intrusions from people. More so, in this age of social media where everyone wants to talk to you and in the end only distract you from doing useful work.

For many of us, resisting intrusions and saying no is practically difficult. We say yes to many things, even things that do not have any beneficial effect on us whatsoever because we want to be liked, we don't want to be rude, we want to be seen as team players, we want to feel a sense of inclusion or we don't want to hurt others (but we end up hurting ourselves).

Whatever your reasons for saying no are, the issue still remains that saying yes to many things can leave you overwhelmed and counterproductive. If your plate is full all the time, then you can't have the space to take on unexpected or ideal opportunities. Suffice to say that if you don't have a strong fence, then everyone will come in and ruin your party.

Here are a few ways to you can build a stronger fence to build a stronger resistance to future distractions in your life.

Make sure you implement a time-delay in your response to requests. Make sure that before accepting an invitation whether professional or personal, you give yourself a little time to think about it. Think about what benefit you stand to gain. Is it worth your time and effort? Is it something you really want to do? What are you giving up in the process? For example, if you receive an invitation and it is something you can do, you can politely say, "Thank you for inviting me, let me check my calendar,

I'll give you a feedback tomorrow." But if it isn't something you want to do, don't be afraid to say something like. "Oh! Thanks for the invitation but I can't do that right now, however, I would love to be involved in the future. I hope you will keep me in mind when another opportunity shows up."

When saying no, learn to say it with authority and grace. If you've thought about an invitation deeply and your answer is no, make sure to decline gracefully while putting your foot down. Here's an example of how to say it without getting yourself into unnecessary tangles of guilt and excuses.

You want to decline: "I appreciate your invitation but I'm afraid I will not be able to (insert what the request is) due to my commitments but I really appreciate your thinking about me."

If you are pressed further by whoever is inviting you, say, "I have high-priority engagements and I simply won't be able to dump or relegate them."

Do not offer a way-out, maybes or even half-steps and specifics. You don't also need to lie. When you say you have commitments, you do! And that's not a lie.

Also, don't over commit yourself. Don't be on the boards of too many committees, organizations, etc. Commitments in themselves do not have any intrinsic value. If it doesn't make you happy and you aren't benefiting from it in one way or the other, then resign from it. Ensure that your commitments are meaningful and worth your effort.

Reduce your meetings. Meetings are a great consumer of time and not all meetings are really important. If you don't need to be at a meeting, then don't show up. Only attend meetings where the coordinator will stick to the agenda and not make unnecessary deviations.

When you set boundaries, keep to them. For example, if you have set apart 6pm to 8pm as your mediation, study, or relaxation period, make sure people know that you are unavailable and inaccessible during that period. Do not answer calls or texts during that period. If colleague contact you in the evenings and on weekends, train yourself to not take their calls or respond to their texts. When you get back, you can say something like that, "I'm sorry I wasn't available to take your call. I'm usually engaged during that period and don't take calls unless it is an emergency."

We teach people how we want them to treat us and so it is important to teach them about respecting our boundaries too.

To be able to achieve your personal goals, you must be able to shun distractions so that you can grow. This means that you must be able to separate the things that will help you reach that goal from the things that will only draw you back. You should grasp the culture of saying no when an offer is bound to be disadvantageous to you and won't move you closer to your goal. Learn to be purposeful and graceful in your approach so that saying no to distractions can be very easy for you.

DAY 14:

LEARNING TO FORGIVE

Forgiveness is hard and it doesn't matter whether it's your boss who denied you promotion after several years of service, or your unfaithful significant other, or a parent who didn't fulfill his or her parental responsibilities to you as a child, or a friend who broadcasted in public something you shared to him or her in confidentiality. We all must carry the burden of whether to forgive and how to forgive at certain points in lives.

When someone does something wrong to you and the initial surge of emotion dissipates, a new challenge faces you and that's the question of whether to forgive the person and move on. By forgiving the person that has wronged you, you are letting go of the heavy burden of grievances, malice and judgements and allowing your heart go through a healing process. But this is very easy to say in principle. In practicality, it could be extremely difficult. But to be able to really forgive, you must understand a few things about forgiveness and common misconceptions that makes it difficult for people to let go and heal.

Forgiveness doesn't mean you are pardoning the person who has wronged you neither does it mean you should tell the person in question that they have been forgiven. Forgiveness doesn't also mean your feelings about the situation when you thought about it, should be indifferent. It doesn't mean that you shouldn't work out anything else in the relationship because you have forgiven the offender.

When you forgive someone, it doesn't mean you should forget what they have done to you neither does it mean you should continue to include them in your life after the negative incident. But by forgiving someone, you are accepting the reality of what happened and you are finding a way to live with it.

This process can be gradual, difficult and doesn't necessarily have to include the person whom you are forgiving. Forgiveness is something you do for yourself not for the person that has wronged you. But if forgiveness is supposed to heal you, why then is it so hard?

There are lots of reasons for that. A major reason for that is when you are wronged, naturally, you will want to seek retribution and avenge the wrong done to you because you have identified yourself as the victim of a wrongdoing and the adrenaline that the anger brings with it is so much you can't get off it. Secondly, you might not want to forgive because that means you run the 'risk' of connecting with the person again. But you can get these feelings resolved when you take the time to understand yourself; your thoughts, your feelings, and your needs.

So now that you have a clearer idea of what forgiveness is and isn't, ask yourself: Am I ready to forgive?

Forgiveness involves the willingness to forgive. The truth is you won't always feel the need to forgive especially if the incident hurt you deeply or the person was abusive or never even showed signs of regret over his or her action. Therefore, until you have fully identified, fully felt, expressed, and flushed out the feeling of anger and pain, only then should you make the attempt to forgive.

1. Think over the incident that made you angry

You must accept that the incident has happened. You must also accept the way it made you feel. If you got rejected by someone you love, don't deny that it made you feel bad or used. Admit the feeling because in order to forgive, you must accept the reality of what has happened and how it affected you.

2. Shift your thoughts to the other person

You must understand that this person is flawed as all humans are. They probably acted from their own level of wisdom, belief, or frame of reference. When you were hurt, did the other person state the reason why they hurt you? Why did they act the way they acted? Doing this doesn't mean you are trying to justify their actions. You are only trying to have an insight as to why the situation went chaotic.

3. Decide if it makes sense to you to tell the person that wronged you that you have forgiven him or her.

Remember that you are not obliged to do this. If you decide not to tell the person that you have forgiven them, then don't. Take the path of forgiveness on your own. Say the words, "I forgive you," aloud. Repeat it as many times as you want until you find inner peace.

In conclusion, forgiveness lets the trauma of what happened to you fade away slowly. You will still remember the wrongdoing but will no longer be chastised by it. Because you have worked through the feelings and learned to be at peace with yourself while strengthening your boundaries, you will be able to prevent such occurrences in the future which is what matters. The act of forgiveness is very effective in reducing one of the numerous baggage we drag through our lives. It is a nice way to elevate and honor yourself while at the same time proving to yourself and others that you decide to be happy.

DAY 15:

ACQUIRE COURAGE AND BE BOLDER

Many of us envy others who are bolder and more courageous and wish we could be like them. We all want to say what we feel the way we want it without appearing like a bully to others. But because this is oftentimes quite difficult to do, we try to water down our thoughts and speech to appear nice and in the end, our message has zero impact.

But being bold is not something you just pull out of your hat like a magic trick and it's not something you just become a guru at overnight. You can only be bolder if you develop an attitude of speaking out your mind in your everyday life. Otherwise, you won't become bold. Here are some thoughts that can help you become bolder in your everyday life.

1. Stop playing too nice

You must understand that not everyone in the world will like you even if you put yourself on an altar and offer yourself as a sacrifice. There will be detractors. There will be people who will feel strongly about you, positively and negatively and others who are indifferent about you. If you want to be bolder and more courageous, you must try to downplay how the feelings of others affect you.

If someone is doing something you don't like or that's causing you to feel negatively, it is better if you stand up and speak up so an end will be put to it instead of trying to avoid confrontation and suffering in silence.

2. Push yourself to talk more (when you have something to say) in groups

Do you restrain yourself from speaking your mind at group meeting because you want to make sure that your contribution is perfect and supported by evidence? Don't waste your time! Research shows that those who speak up more in groups are perceived as leaders.

That just makes sense because standing up to share your thoughts in a group especially when the members of the group are people you are unfamiliar with puts a target on you and subjects you to immediate passive evaluation by other group members even when they are not evaluating your contribution—and that requires courage. Since people tend to generally gravitate towards courageous people, they perceive them to have other leadership traits too.

3. Think about the worst thing that can happen (but still go ahead)

Sometimes, we want to really stand up and say something bold but we often stay silent because of a nameless disaster that will happen if we do. But if you think it through and ask yourself, "What's the worst thing that could happen?" You will then realize that the outcome is not as bad as you've initially thought it to be. Perhaps, he will only be upset for a few hours but you would have told him something that on deeper introspection will help him later in life. Can you handle it? Yes, you can! But you will discover that if you actually say what you really want to say, he might not even get upset for five minutes. He will only thank you for being straight forward. Often times, the consequences we anticipate never really happen.

4. Build momentum

Your path to courage is not a one-time thing. You must try at creating series of actions that will improve your confidence, speed, and power. You must keep up appearance, show up, and be visible to the people that surround you. If you have a plan that's going to be helpful to someone, muster everything within you to tell them. You never can tell who your ideas can help and people never forget how you make them feel especially if you come up with a solution that's been giving them a hard time.

Therefore, take advantage of any opportunity to be helpful and visible. Don't belittle any situation that earns your attention, respect and popularity. It is on these pedestals that you can gradually improve your courage.

DAY 16:

MANAGE YOUR ANGER MORE EFFECTIVELY

Anger needs no introduction because it is something that we all feel from time to time whether as a mild annoyance or a full-fledge rage. It is completely normal, occasionally healthy, and a human emotion. But if it persists and continues to grow unchecked, then it becomes a serious concern and could be very destructive—at work, at home in personal relationships and the overall quality of the life of the person beset by it. The instinctive and natural way to express anger is by showing aggression. As a natural and adaptive way to respond to threats, it usually inspires feelings that are strong, powerful and usually leads us to fight or defend ourselves from an aggressor.

Therefore, it is safe to say that a certain level of anger is important for the survival of a person. Even though, uncontrolled anger tends to lead to destruction of the self and inanimate objects, yet, unexpressed anger is a problem. It can morph into more pathological cases of anger such as passive- aggressive behavior, insulting people indirectly without telling them what they've done wrong, or the development of a personality that seems to be hostile and cynical. From the foregoing, it is not surprising that those who haven't learnt the proper way to express anger often have unsuccessful relationships with others. If you fall into this category, there is help on the way. You can find a way to calm down the storm that wells up in you each time you are provoked. You can also learn how to control your outward behavior and internal responses, taking sure steps to reduce your heart rate and let the feelings of anger in you subside very quickly.

First of all, you must be able to use relaxation strategies such as deep breathing and relaxing images to help you calm your nerves. Here are simple techniques you can try out.

- Breathe in deeply from the bottom of your chest
- Slowly repeat a calming phrase like "take it easy," or "You don't need to get so angry" as many times as you can to help you calm down
- Visualize a moment in your life; probably from past memories, where you were very happy
- Engage in non-strenuous exercises like Yoga to help you relax your mind

The key is to be able to remember and practice these techniques as many times as you can when you get into a situation that makes you angry.

Secondly, you need to also change the way you think. Some people, when angry, tend to heap insults, curses, and use other negative words that reflect their inner thoughts. This shouldn't be you. You must learn the act of self-restraint when verbally expressing your anger so you don't say things that you will later regret after you calm down. Instead of raising your voice at someone saying, "You keep forgetting things," a statement that makes you feel justified and humiliate the other person who might initially be doing his or her best to make sure a solution is provided to the problem you seek. You can say, "I told you this earlier…this is what I mean…" You must also understand that logic trumps anger all the time, because anger, even when it is justified, can become very irrational as soon as you subject it to logic. So every time you are about to reach your flash point and explode, remind yourself that no one is out to make you angry but disappointments happens and it is part of those rough patches one is bound to come in contact with when going through life. Doing this lets you get a more balanced perspective on things.

Often times, when you are angry, leaving your immediate environment is usually the best solution to avoid dissipating the irritation and fury that's welling up in you. Take a break, take a walk and go make out some personal time for yourself.

Whatever happens, if you are capable of taking just a second to analyze a situation that's boiling without reacting impulsively, then you'll be better capable of handling an irritating situation.

DAY 17:

IMPROVE YOUR SPIRITUAL LIFE

Contrary to the popular and misguided belief that living a spiritual life is living a life of addiction to incense, trips to India, visits to the Dalai Lama, genuflecting at a temple of Buddha and having a guru, a Sensei, or a Rabbi on speed dial, being a spiritual person is nothing like that. Spiritual living isn't some level of living that is accessible to most of us. Spiritual living is accessible to everyone whether you believe in angels, destiny, goddesses, God, spirit or tooth fairies!

Spiritual growth is the process of awakening and becoming conscious of our inner self. It is the elevation of your inner being beyond the ordinary level of existence into awakening into some universal truths. It is the realization of who you truly are. Spiritual growth is a process by which we leave misconceptions, wrong thoughts, belief systems and ideas while becoming more conscious of who we truly are. And it is very important to everyone because it forms the basis for a life that is free of tension, fear, and anxiety and one that is full of harmony.

By going on a journey of self-transformation, your view to life changes. You'll learn not to let outer distractions affect your inner being and state of mind. You will exude composure and detachment and develop inner power and strength, all of which are very important to your being and relationship with others. Spiritual growth does not mean you will start behaving strangely or irrationally or abscond from your responsibilities and become an impractical and illogical person. It only means you will understand yourself better and stay away from situations or activities that will leave you dejected, unhappy, and bitter.

Spiritual growth is not a means for escaping from responsibilities, behaving strangely and becoming an impractical person. It doesn't also mean a life of seclusion. It is only a way of growing and becoming a stronger, happier and more responsible person. You can grow your business, spend time with your family and still engage in activities that will elevate you spiritually.

You can walk on the path of spiritual growth, and at the same time live the same kind of life as everyone else. You do not have to live a secluded life in some faraway place or monastery. You can raise a family, work or run a business, and yet at the same time engage in practices that lead to inner growth.

You can start growing your spiritual life by reading spiritual and uplifting books. Take breaks to ponder on what you have learnt and see where in your life you can apply it. Also, set apart a fraction of your day to meditate and involve yourself in concentration exercises.

You can also grow your spiritual life by taking hold of your inner chatter and making it healthier. You must recognize and pick out your negative chatter like endless whining and complaining. Ascending spiritually is about trusting in the path of your life and understanding that there is goodness and evil in people and it's your job to know how to use both to a positive advantage for you. Purging your mind of negative thinking is very important if you want to connect with your higher self.

Most religions recommend that you treat other people the way you would want from Christianity to Buddhism. Why don't you just try that for just half a day? Smile at someone you ordinarily can't stand. Offer to do grocery shopping for a senior in the adjacent apartment. Attempt to be patient, generous, and thoughtful. Let others in your lane when driving. Put someone ahead of you. Spiritual growth is about being attuned with our positive self in thought and in deed. If you want to grow, offer out love and watch as the world becomes better than it was five minutes ago.

Decide to have faith. This is often difficult for self-professed logical thinkers because faith is simply illogical. Faith is simply believing that something positive and powerful will happen to you. But to climb to a higher level of spiritual growth, you must be willing to take leaps of faith from time to time. This will help you get rid of unnecessary worry and affirm your confidence in the action that you've taken.

Spiritual growth is accessible to anyone that desires a life of happiness and peace. What differs from individual to individual is the ease with which the inner self can be awaken and this is dependent on the weight of thoughts, belief system and negative habits that is placed on it.

DAY 18:

LEARNING TO CO-OPERATE BETTER WITH OTHERS

The question as to whether humans are naturally cooperative or not is one that no one has been able to really answer—and this is good. Why is this good, you ask? Co-operating with others is not as simple as ABC. It requires keeping to complex rules like constitutions for unions and other societies, marriage vows and agreeing to terms and conditions if you want to get hired by an organization. The best form of co-operation is where you work with someone who is good at your weakness and terrible at your strength.

But often times, this rarely happens and that's why, people getting fired from jobs and getting divorced are hugely popular. Mutual self-interest is what drives successful co-operation; a relationship survives as long as the parties involved are benefitting. But then, the scales are never balanced in most relationships. One party benefits more while the other person sacrifices or compromises more to make sure the relationship thrives.

For example, the way most small businesses are set up one person (the boss) does things the way he wants while others in the company do things the way the boss wants. Your salary is then dependent on how good you are at doing the things he wants. But since we won't always be entrepreneurs or have things done our way, we will often find ourselves in situations where we can't simply do things our way and therefore have to compromise and work with others to achieve a common objective. In such situations, it helps to keep a few things regarding working with others in mind.

One of them is to prepare ahead for potential criticisms. This will allow you to have an appropriate response available should it happen that the criticism surfaces. Therefore, when Cousin Margaret comes over on Christmas day and says it looks like you have gained belly fat and offers you a way out, thank her for her observation and kind gesture and move on to another topic.

You must also realize that since every human being has a different outlook on life, it pays to play the devil's advocate every once in a while. If you try to look at things from other people's perspective, you will realize that situations and conversations that can be potentially rough and tacky can be smooth.

When someone says something that doesn't sit well with you, before you act, stop and take few slow deep breaths to allow you to decompress and then iron out the issue with the other party. When you do this more often, you will realize that most times, people aren't out to hurt or malign you and immediately you understand this, the fog oftentimes clear up.

Cultivate an air of positivity. People who are calm, good-natured, polite, considerate, attentive, and who dressed well, are usually perceived as charming and attractive. Therefore, learn to create an air of positivity around yourself. Dress well, accept and give compliments, be pleasant and always learn to smile. Practice these skills and let them become second-nature to you.

A passage of the Holy Bible, Proverbs 15:1 says that, "A soft answer turns away wrath, but grievous words stir up anger." So you can see that it doesn't really make sense for you to fuel a conflict just because you want to allow your ego the satisfaction of reacting when provoked. Instead of escalating a conflict and robbing yourself of inner joy and peace, use every opportunity to depressurize the situation. You can leave the scene when the pressure reaches a point you can't handle and return later. But if you are involved in one in which you can't leave immediately, then do your best to defuse the situation.

In conclusion, understand that there is a very good chance that the problem might not even be others; that it might be you. So look within and ask others for feedback periodically. It is easy for us to see a speck in the eyes of others but blind to the log of wood sitting in the corner of our very own eyes. Therefore, be humble, be true to yourself and continue to work at being the ultimate version of yourself.

DAY 19:

FIND INSPIRATION EVERY DAY

If you engage in a particular routine every day, for example, you take the route to the train station to work, pass the same house, the same heap of trash, the same cars, etc. It is just a matter of time before life itself starts to look lifeless and dull because of the feeling that there's nothing else to see. Even though, this is not true, the mundaneness would have already dulled your shine and stifled your creativity.

But if you take an alternate route and deliberately look out for what has changed since the last time you took it, your mood lightens up and the small exploration will make your mundane walk very exciting. To find inspiration, improve your creativity, and produce lot of new ideas, you can follow these steps.

Grow your curiosity. How do you this? By making efforts to notice new details. You will find that the more you pay attention to the details around you, the more you will discover new things and will want to explore.

Learn to step back from all the craziness of your day's activities and do something pleasurable even unconventional, like going out in the rain or snow. *Take a walk in the Park*. Go bowling with family etc. Go fishing, just do things that are very fulfilling and exciting!

Weigh the pros and cons to balance yourself and discover relaxation. This act of little challenge can often set into motion a strong cycle of inspirational thoughts with unquantifiable value.

Break cycle once in a while. When you are programmed to take your kids to school before 7am, sign in at work at 8am, yoga at 6pm, meetings at 8pm—living a regimented life—everything tends to become very dull and fun-deprived. Therefore, on some occasions, break that cycle because un-programmed exercise and exploration of things like school, workplaces, gadgets have been known to revitalize the mind and offer far greater rewards than any posted by physical exercise.

Be deliberate about noticing the small things around you. Go out of your way to read a book on a niche area that you have little or no knowledge about. This doesn't mean that you should totally disrupt the order of your life. It is a gradual shift and exploration is second nature.

Share your big dream with a friend. Talk to a friend about what you would like to do one day. Think about it deeply and visualize every detail as much as you can. If you don't have a friend, you can talk to about this, then write everything out on a list. Doing this will give you inspiration and ideas will start flowing in.

Do something fun outside of your work or recurrent tasks. It doesn't have to be every day of the week, even if it is once a week. Go to a rock concert, watch a game, go visit a friend or relation staying in another state, visit the public library, or just have a night out with the guys or girls.

DAY 20:

TRANSFORM YOURSELF TO A BETTER LISTENER

Research has shown that we rarely remember anything more than 25% of what we hear—and this poses a problem. It can affect generally the way we communicate with the people in our social and professional circles.

Developing the ability to really listen and internalize words, not just hearing what is being said, is of paramount importance in building stronger ties to the people in our social circle and network.

One of the best tactics to employ when you want to really listen, to get what's being communicated beyond what's being said, is to look at the speaker and maintain eye contact during the length of the conversation. If you find that looking at the other person in the eye for an extended period makes you uncomfortable, you can look at a corner of their face or their nose.

The most important thing is to get your eye level directly on their face. As you do this, make sure to look out for non-verbal cues. Are they smiling as they are narrating how they got involved in an accident? Are they making hand gestures to better explain something to you? You should also pay attention to your body language too. If you are trying to suppress a smile as your speaker is narrating how a woman got hit by a large bus as she is crossing the highway, then your action might be taken as a lack of empathy.

If you are slouched in your sit, arms crossed across your chest, then you are subtly communicating that you are not feeling the conversation and would rather watch paint dry! Therefore, sit upright, lean forward, and do your best to maintain eye contact from time to time.

If the speaker was saying something you don't completely understand, seek clarification. Don't attempt to read their minds. Ask open-ended questions that will allow the reader to explain themselves better, instead of a question that will allow them to give an ordinary 'yes' or 'no'. Reading someone's mind is difficult, don't kid yourself that you can do it efficiently all of the time.

On the same side of the coin, if you don't completely agree with the speaker, be civil about it. Don't make rude interruptions. Allow the person to completely finish what they intend to communicate. Don't listen to give a reply. Listen to get the speaker's point. Anticipating the other person's point even before it is being said is a very bad communication strategy; the same is preparing a rebuttal mid-way into the other person's speech. Wait until the person is done before formulating your response, if you are going to disagree, do it tactfully and respectfully.

Keep your smartphone and other distractions away. Browsing the internet, doing dishes, or responding to a Twitter notification when trying to listen often makes you miss out some important details which you would have otherwise found useful. In fact, it might even make the other person feel like what they are saying is unimportant since what they have, is your divided attention. So, put down that phone while listening and focus on the discussion at hand.

You should also learn to paraphrase or summarize what the other person has said from time to time during your discussion. For example, "Are you saying Britain's exit from the EU will cause the Pound to weaken?" Paraphrasing has the ability to encourage the speaker and it will prove that you've been listening to what they've been saying all along. This will also give them the opportunity to clarify any grey area in the discussion.

Lastly, be open about your current limitations. If you have to quickly get to attend to something and would not be able to listen for a while longer, it is best to let the speaker be aware. If you are stressed and your mind needs to go on a break, then ensure to let the speaker understand your predicament. It is best to continue the conversation later than try to fake undivided attention when it is not working out for you.

DAY 21:

WORK ON YOUR COMPASSION

What does it mean to be compassionate? Compassion is that feeling of empathy or sympathy that you have towards another person in need. It is that feeling of shared suffering or shared grief.

Compassion is part of what makes us human. It is that feeling that comes from the depth of our soul when we compare ourselves to another human in need or suffering. True compassion can never be faked.

A quote attributed to Frederick Buechner goes, "compassion is sometimes the fatal capacity for feeling what it is like to live inside somebody else's skin. It is the knowledge that there can never really be any peace and joy for me until there is peace and joy finally for you too."

Being compassionate is beneficial in the sense that by helping others, we help ourselves too. We tend to get a positive feeling after doing good which can lead to contentment and peace.

If you want others to be happy, practice compassion. If you want to be happy, practice compassion. – Dalai Lama

Before you get to work on being more compassionate, it's important that you understand a few things about compassion. First, you must understand that compassion is a gradual process and is not something that will happen to you all of a sudden. You must also know that compassion is not something you will achieve in a day or a week. It will take time, effort and resolution and you will begin to see changes in your thought process as you grow more compassionate.

So how do you become more compassionate?

The first step is to actually learn how to listen to people. Learning to listen to people has been discussed extensively in Day 21. As you are listening, suspend all judgement and give the person your attention. Don't attempt to formulate replies in your mind nor wait for a lull in the discussion to pass your opinion. There is powerful healing in you being able to share your darkest secrets to someone and them not judging you. As the person is speaking, try to respond to the emotion and not the words. Angry words sometimes conceal fear and people often blame others when in fact they are the guilty ones. It's a human thing.

Secondly, you must understand that suffering is universal. We would have at some point in our lives suffered from something. A broken relationship. An abusive partner. A wicked boss. A high school bully. The death of a loved one. The loss of a job. The list is endless. The particular details may be different but the theme is universal across continents and traditions. So it pays to call your memory back to the time when you or someone close to you went through something similar. Bring yourself back to that moment. How did it make you feel? Meditate on this and remind yourself of every emotion you went through and how much you hoped for a comforter and empathy from someone. Do this often and you will gradually become more compassionate.

If someone you know is taking a downward spiral along a negative path, it is easy for you to forget their positive qualities. Make it a point to always call yourself back to the point when they used to have a particular strength that you used to admire. They may be hard working, loyal, funny, hopeful, patient, etc. Visualize the person from their positive perspective, this will help you be more compassionate towards them.

If you have never gone through the pain someone went through, it might not be easy for you to be compassionate. But when you take a step back and put yourself in their shoes. Imagine what you would do, if you were in their situation. How would you want to be comforted? How would you want others to treat you? It pays to treat other people the way you would also want to be treated and this is not just a cliché, it is what you need to do to be more compassionate.

Lastly, know that you won't always feel compassionate towards everybody going through one form of pain or the other. You will fail to be compassionate towards people that truly needs your compassion from time to time. You are not perfect. No one is. You are going through your own issues too, it is understandable. As long as your intentions and efforts are directed in the right path most times, everything will work out well in the end.

DAY 22:

ACHIEVE EMOTIONAL INDEPENDENCE

One of the greatest feelings in the world is one of total emotional independence. A life lived in emotional independence is one in which your mood, self-esteem, and self-worth are controlled entirely by you and not by anything like your friends, thoughts, the society's expectation or statutes dictated by parents or others who have some level of control over you. It is having feelings that are independent of the thought and opinions of others. It is deciding to choose your emotional responses to life's circumstances.

You can achieve emotional independence by reframing the past. Whatever it is you faced in the past, no matter the difficulties you went through in your last marriage or while growing up, you can reframe it now and change what it means to you now. You can change the message: whether it is abuse, poor parenting that has led you to believe that you are not loveable or can't amount to anything in life. You can change those messages, you can throw them in the trash can and completely change the story you have engraved on your mind. You must purge yourself of feelings of shame, guilt, and feelings of worthlessness and replace them with more accurate interpretation of parental inadequacy, abuse, etc.

Then move to the forgiveness phase, where you will free yourself of the people that have held you in this current state that you have found yourself. If your uncle neglected you when you needed him the most, you must forgive him and see him as a human being who is flawed and weak in his own way. That way, you free yourself from the anchor of the past: the hate, guilt and anger that has locked you down this long. When you do this, you will start to feel the more subdued emotional response of pity or compassion (as discussed in day 21) for the lives of unhappiness that they themselves must have lived. You are doing this not to absolve them of their negative actions on you but to enable you to understand the emotional context in which they acted. Think about the story of Jesus Christ, Mandela, and Gandhi as they were all beaten and jailed and were still able to rise above the sufferings to forgive the people who treated them badly. This won't be an easy step especially if you suffered in the hands of your own biological parents, but you can find peace if you truly wanted it.

Next, find yourself. The more you try to go on a path of self-discovery, the less outside forces can make you feel less than you truly know yourself to be. Tell yourself every day that you are a remarkable human with the infinite potential of attracting positive situations and things. You are beautiful and carefully created with high value. You are born to make positive and significant impact and radiates light that suppresses the parental inadequacies, abuse, stupidity, meanness, etc. You are who you choose to be and not what your friends say you are. Never accept what other people perceive you to be. You are who you say you are.

Accept who you are. With this definition of who you are, ensure you internalize it. Don't wait for others opinion of an idea before promoting it yourself. Do not get offended when someone says they don't like you or have a negative opinion about the kind of job you do. It is what you think of yourself that matters and you must continue to internalize and radiate this.

Finally, work on personal growth and development. You are currently not the best version of yourself. There is still a higher level of growth you should aspire to. Being stagnant will not earn you respect but continuous growth will. You must look at the areas where you think you are flawed by stepping back and taking an objective look at your life. You can also do this by asking for feedback from people that you trust. What is your passion? How can you keep the fire burning? Do you speak well in public? How can you work on that? Are you shy or find every opportunity to avoid confrontation? Why is that? How can you get better? As you take steps to improve yourself in your flawed areas, you will become less dependent on the thought of others towards you and what you are doing.

DAY 23:

GET ENOUGH SLEEP TO GET ON TOP OF YOUR DAY

How often you sleep goes a long way in determining how productive your life will be. Your sleep schedule, habits around bedtime, daily activities, and lifestyle choice all play important roles in determining the quality of the rest you get and, by extension, your productivity. Health practitioners usually recommend that as an adult, you need between six to eight hours of sleep to get on top of your activities and this time range can make a lot of difference in your mental alertness, emotional balance and level of energy that you need to carry you through the day.

One of the most important strategies for achieving good sleep is getting in sync with your body's natural sleep-wake cycle. It helps to stick to a regular sleep schedule. It will make you feel really refreshed and energized. Keeping a consistent schedule is very important and you can achieve that by setting a realistic bedtime that will work for you depending on factors like role in the family, job, and lifestyle.

Another effective strategy is to control your exposure to light. Your body secretes more of a hormone called melatonin, when it's dark, which causes you to sleep and less when there is light, making you more alert.

However, your lifestyle choice can alter the natural production of this hormone and can result in irregular sleep cycle. Therefore, at nights, avoid staring at bright screens within 2 hours of your bedtime. This applies to your phone, tablets, computer, or TV. If you cannot do this, ensure you reduce the brightness of the software that can automatically adjust the color of your display. When it's actually time to sleep, ensure the room is dark. The darker it is, the better you will sleep. If you feel the light is important for your security, then use a sleep mask to cover your eyes and cover any electronics that can emit light like the digital clock on your bed side table.

You might also want to consider what you eat. Your daytime eating habit can definitely affect how well you will sleep at night. For a start, you might want to first reduce your caffeine intake. Caffeine has been known to cause sleep problems from ten to up to twelve hours after it has been consumed. Also, if you are going to bed at 10pm, ensure you are done eating dinner at 8pm especially if it is a heavy meal containing some significant level of fats and carbohydrate as your body needs more time to break them down for digestion to take place and this might make you twist and turn in bed.

You should also avoid consuming acidic foods very close to bed time so they don't cause heartburn. Avoid taking alcohol before bed too. And as far as food is concerned, avoid taking too many liquids so your sleep won't be disrupted by excessive bathroom breaks in the night.

If you make an extra effort of making your environment conducive, you have a better chance of sleeping well. A few things you can do is reduce the noise entering your bedroom. If you can't stand the sound of barking dogs, loud neighbors, traffic or other people milling around in your house, then try by masking those annoying sounds with your fan or white noise. A white noise is a consistent noise that comes out evenly across all hearing frequencies and has been scientifically proven to induce sleep. You can buy a sound machine or make your own white noise by setting your radio to a frequency that is between two radio stations. If this doesn't help, use an ear plug. If your problem is not the noise, try varying the temperature of your room. Most people find it easier to sleep in a slightly cool room with temperatures of, say, 65 Fahrenheit. Ensure to also check your bed covers and mattress. If you wake up in the morning with an aching neck or sore back, then try a different mattress or different pillows.

Finally, you can indulge in a few bedtime habits and activities such as, reading a book or magazine using soft light, taking a cold bath, listening to slow music, doing some easy stretches, listening to audio books, and making plans for the following day. These activities have been known to make people unwind and sleep better at night.

DAY 24:

DEALING WITH GRIEF

Grief is the natural response to the loss of something we hold dear to us. These loses include the loss of a job, the death of someone we hold dear or the physical separation from someone, or something, close to us, the loss of property to disaster or even something like retirement or dishonorable discharge from the armed forces. It is simply the loss of something dear to us and it can be experienced by anyone. But everyone grieves differently; that is to say people react and cope with this feeling of loss in different ways. Some have a healthy response mechanism while others react negatively when experiencing grief. The acknowledgment of the fact that it is normal to grieve, allows someone to mourn a loss and then heal.

There are different stages of grief that an individual tends to undergo and they are highlighted below.
1. Denial: In this stage, you try to protect yourself from the shocking news and might become inactive or numb taking time to fully process what has been experienced. For example, in the loss of a loved one, people have been known to go through a period of disbelief where they do not try to accept the fact that their loved ones are dead. But as time passes, they will fully acknowledge the loss only then will denial and disbelief tend to diminish.

2. Bargaining: In this stage, you tend to think about the many things you could have done to prevent the loss. If this feeling is not resolved, they can be drawn back by feelings of guilt and remorse and this may interfere with the healing process.
3. Depression: This stage occurs when you fully accept the true extent of the loss and what it could mean for you going forward. In this stage, people tend to go through lack of sleep and appetite, lethargy, lack of concentration and lots of crying spells. You may feel lonely, empty, and isolated.
4. Anger: This is the fourth stage and occurs from feelings of helplessness. It can result from a feeling of abandonment caused by a loved one's death. A grieving individual may be angry at a higher power or just towards life in general.
5. Acceptance: Over time, you may be able to come to agreement with the fact that the loss is never going to be restored and this is the only time when true healing starts to take place. Healing can start immediately the loss becomes integrated into the individual's set of life experiences. Understand that throughout a person's lifetime, they may from time to time go back to the earlier stages of grief. There is no time limit to the grieving process and each individual will have to set and plan their own healing process.

How to cope with grief.

The first step to overcoming grief is to know that it is alright to feel weak, helpless and cry. It is perfectly normal and you shouldn't try to stifle the feeling. You must understand that even though you can succeed at suppressing grief, you cannot avoid it forever. In order to heal, you must acknowledge the pain. Avoiding the feeling will only result in feelings of depression, anxiety, and other health problems. As you are going through this process of acceptance, ensure that you don't go through it alone. Find a support group. Talk to a family member. Go to your church or temple. Let someone know you are grieving but don't let them tell you how to feel. Do it your own way. Your grief is yours to feel. Also, you must understand that in future there will be triggers: anniversaries, holidays and milestones that will open up your memories and make you feel down. This is all perfectly normal. It doesn't mean you are weak.

Secondly, you must look after your health, avoid being alone or using antidepressants or getting involved in hard drugs and alcohol. But, instead, find a longer lasting solution like trying to be in the company of friends or families, writing out your feelings in a journal, going outdoors, looking for other people who are going through a similar situation or seeking the support of a professional counselor.

DAY 25:

TAKE GRATITUDE MORE SERIOUSLY

Human needs are never satiated, and with a lot of things going on in our lives every day, it is very easy to take a lot of things for granted. You drive a Volkswagen but want a Porsche Cayenne but take for granted the gift of having limbs to drive them. You need a bigger house to accommodate your growing family but never have been thankful for the sound health they are enjoying. You want a post graduate degree but never thankful for the gift of being alive and able to even earn a first degree. We complain about the economy, government's policy, climate change and never truly undergo self-introspection to reflect on the seemingly little things that we take for granted but means so much to others and could be the game changer for them. Today, we must throw out that feeling of ingratitude and begin to reflect on the little things that we have that oils our lives and make things easier for us. This can be done by

1. Keeping a gratitude diary: Each day, you must remind yourself of the gifts, benefits, undeserved kindness and other good things of life that you currently enjoy. Taking out time to personally reflect on the beauties of ordinary moments, your life's journey and how far you have come, and the people in your life that you love and care about

can help you become more grateful for where you are in life and give you the assurance that you aren't doing bad in life because it could actually be worse.
2. Saying the word "Thank you" often. By communicating more verbally how you appreciate the people that bring happiness into your life, you are indirectly lighting up your own life. We all love to be appreciated, no matter who we are. So the next time, someone leaves the door open for you, learn to thank them for their kindness. Being grateful for the little things will make you more appreciative of the big things when they eventually come.
3. Volunteering to help others. Research has shown that people who regularly engage in volunteer activity stand a lower risk of depression and tend to be generally happier. Getting involved in disaster relief programs, food aids for people in countries plagued by drought to general charity work like rescuing lost animals can help you find inspiration and fully appreciate your own life and the things that will make it run smoothly for you.
4. Praying more often. Many religions like Christianity considers prayers involving gratitude the best of prayers. Why? Because this type of prayers make the followers recognize and remain properly attached to the ultimate source of all they are and will ever be.
5. Spending more time with nature. It really helps to be able to see the wonders around you because this will truly make you appreciate nature and its beauty. Being outside will help give your brain the break it deserves and rid yourself of depressing thoughts that can tend to leave you with feelings of ingratitude. When your body functions really well, your mind will tend to follow suit.

6. Remembering the bad moments in your life. To be grateful for where you are right now, it helps to remember the hard times you've gone through in the past or that you once experienced. When you take the time to ponder on what used to be a few years back and how far you have been successful in navigating life's challenges, you are able to set up an explicit contrast in your mind and this contrast becomes the canvass on which you can paint the image of your gratitude.

7. Not comparing yourself to others. This one could be quite difficult especially seeing that the world we live in today is pervaded with images of wealth, fast cars, perfect body figures, etc. and we seem to find them everywhere we turn. But dwelling on other people's wealth and beauty has not really helped anybody. Instead, it helps to focus on your beauty, how magnificent you are and how blessed you have been. You have a rewarding career, you are about to get a degree, you have loving parents, you are surrounded by caring children, you have the respect of people in your church, your friends consider you smart, you consider yourself smart and good-looking and you have so much to offer the world. You must take the time to evaluate the good things that you have in your own life.

DAY 26:

UNDERSTAND HOW TO MAKE BETTER AND MORE REWARDING DECISIONS

Your success in life, whether in your workplace or personal life, is very dependent on how effective you are at making important decisions. Normally, it could feel overwhelming when you have to think about the number of decisions you would have to make in your lifetime so you can be successful but if you are able to think carefully and carve out effective strategies, your decision making ability can get better and your life will be more manageable and rewarding.

In order to make better decisions, it is important that first of all, you know the outcome of every situation as this will properly enable you to evaluate your strategies to achieve the desired outcome. Your objectives should be well-defined and anticipate future outcomes taking into account all you desire to achieve. Putting down what you want is a crucial and highly important step in achieving your goals. Also, you should think about how the goals you are setting in the interim fit into your larger plans. Perhaps, you have decided to quit your current career line, you must understand what your long-term goal is for your career and think about what actions and strategies can help you to quickly transit to the new career and help you to get the relevant experience and skills so you can move up the ladder real quickly. Also, you must also gather evidences before you make any decisions.

Look out for facts and evidences that will allow you weigh your decisions more objectively.

When you are done and have decided to go forward with a decision, make sure it is time-bound. Perhaps you have decided that you will write the GMAT so you can get into a business school, then you must put time-constraint to it. Any decision that isn't time-bound can drag for so long that you might not eventually execute it. You must also be able to prioritize tasks in addition to appending time limitations. Time and priority are very central to making decisions that are effective and rewarding.

When you have decided on the strategies and decisions that will enable you to achieve a goal, you must ensure to write them down. It is a popular saying that, the faintest ink is better than the sharpest brain. If you don't write things down, you tend to forget and may not be able to execute tasks on a priority basis.

In addition to that, you must allow, in your plan, a flexibility factor that allows you to accommodate unpredictable outcomes. You must consider the unknown variables and unpredictable outcomes.

Anticipating those outcomes can help you evaluate whether or not a possible outcome is worth the risk you are going to take. You must understand that no one is above unforeseen circumstances.

That's why they are called unforeseen circumstances, so it is important that you always have an alternative, should you face a challenge that you might not be able to overcome.

When your plans reach the execution stage, it is important that you make a list of your support system and reach out to them. Tell the people you trust about your plan and seek advice on the issue. Having a support system can help you achieve your objective while reducing the pressure and stress level you might be facing. When you are reaching out for support, don't ask for a validation of your goals but advice. Your aim isn't for people to tell you what you want to hear but instead what you need to achieve your set goals. Ask others that have gone the similar path you plan to take. How did they do it? How can you best prepare yourself? What was it like? When doing this, you must understand that responses may vary and you should have it at the back of your mind that the ultimate decision to follow through is yours. You can ask for advice from the wisest of men but it means nothing if you are not able to follow through.

This brings us to the concluding part, if you have decided to follow through with decision, you must execute tasks by step-wisely and by deadline. Having a deadline allows you to have a better understanding of the issue and know that you've considered the situation thoroughly. So, put your choices into action, now that you have carefully considered every angle of the issue with trusted sources. And as you continue to execute these tasks, examine whether you've made the right decisions. Give yourself performance reviews and ask whether you have made the best decision.

This is not to say you should second-guess or doubt your ability to achieve a goal. It only means that you should have an objective review of your strategy from time to time to see if the course of action taken, is the best you could have and to help you modify the plan if it is not going to help you achieve the set goals.

DAY 27:

EAT HEALTHIER AND MAINTAIN A GOOD DIET

The issue of dieting to maintain weight, gain weight or lose weight is one that everyone who has an access to TV, internet or books is presumably inundated with. We've seen celebrities lose weight rapidly by drinking green tea, we've seen others lose weight by working out, we've seen a friend burn belly fat and build muscles through some hacks he read in a book or internet article so dieting is not a new topic and in this book it won't be treated as such. What exactly is a healthy diet? A healthy diet is a meal that includes the following in the right proportion:

- Protein (present in fish, meat, poultry, dairy products, eggs, nuts, beans, and cowpea)
- Fat (present in animal and dairy products, nuts, and oils)
- Carbohydrates (present in fruits, vegetables, whole grains, and beans and other legumes)
- Vitamins (such as vitamins A, B, C, D, E, and K)
- Minerals (such as calcium, potassium, and iron)
- Water (needs no introduction!)

Whether you are dieting or not, your body needs these classes of food to be able to function more optimally. So how can you do that?

Incorporate greens and fruits in your meal. Choose red, orange and green vegetables like tomatoes, sweet potatoes, and broccoli alongside your meals. Take fruits with your meal to nourish your body with the vitamins, minerals, and fiber your body needs to be healthy and able to fight diseases. If you are going to eat grains, ensure half of the time you are eating whole-grain food. Look out for things like brown rice, oatmeal, wild rice, whole wheat, etc. The idea is to switch from refined grains to whole-grain foods.

Drink more of fat-free or low-fat milk, even though both contain the same amount of calcium and other nutrients as whole milk, they have less saturated fats and as a result are more advantageous. Reduce your calorie intake by drinking lots of water instead of soda drinks. Try adding a slice of lemon or lime in your water if you want some flavor or better still purchase flavored water.

Eat different types of lean protein foods: Meat, poultry, seafood, dry beans or peas, eggs, nuts, and seeds are all members of the protein family. You can also choose leaner cuts of ground beef (where the label reads 90% lean or higher), turkey breast, or chicken breast. Consume more seafood: Seafood includes fish (such as salmon, tuna, and trout) and shellfish (such as crab, mussels, and oysters) and is rich in protein, minerals, and omega-3 fatty acids (heart-healthy fat). Eating at least eight ounces of seafood is bound to do your body a whole lot of good.

If your aim is weight maintenance and you are not looking to drastically increase or reduce your weight, then the following tips will prove very useful.

Find a way to balance calories: Do a search for how many calories you need to pull you through a day as a first step in managing your weight. When you are done, plan, analyze, and track your diet and physical activity using some apps and other guides that are available Also, you should learn to cut back and eat less. Take the time to fully enjoy your food as you eat it. Don't eat too fast or rush your food. Pay attention to hunger and fullness clues before, during, and after meals. Use them as a signal to understand when to eat and when you are full. Reduce your consumption of solid fats.

In conclusion, be physically active and exercise. This cannot be over-emphasized. Being physically active can help you maintain your normal weight. Young people (6-17 years old) need to be active for at least one hour a day while adults (18 and older) need to be active for at least half an hour every day.

DAY 28:

MANAGE STRESS MORE EFFECTIVELY

You may be thinking that you can't do anything about stress. You may be overwhelmed with the thought that the bills won't stop rising, there won't be more hours than 24 in the day to accomplish what you want, and your work and family responsibilities and demands will keep rising. Stress management is all about being in control: of your lifestyle, thoughts, emotions, and the manner with which you handle your challenges. It doesn't matter how stressful your life might appear to be, there are actions you can take to reduce the pressure and take control of the situation.

The first of those solutions is to make sure that you always keep moving. Being physically active can help you reduce stress and you don't have to be an athlete to achieve that. Any form of movement or physical activity that can help your brain depressurize or burn away the anger, tension, and frustration and help boost your mood and make you feel good, can serve as a good source of pressure-release tool for you.

For example, you can put some music on and dance around, take your dog for a walk, walk or take a cycle to the grocery store, decide to use the stairs rather than the elevator, or play video games with your children. The reason this is effective, is that physical activities releases endorphins, that improve your mood and make you feel good and can also be a source of distraction from your worries.

You should also make effort to improve your social connections. If you are feeling stressed, it won't hurt to talk to a colleague at work, help someone else achieve a difficult task, have dinner with friends, follow someone to the cinema or attend a music show, email a longtime friend, go for a walk with a buddy, meet new people and talk to a coach, mentor, or spiritual leader.

Social engagement is highly important and is arguably the quickest and most efficient way to kill stress and avoid being passive-aggressive to people.

Not that the people you talk to necessarily have to be able to fix all your problems, they just need to be able to hear you out. So understand that opening up is not a sign that you are weak and can't handle your problems. In fact, opening up will make people hold you more in high esteem as they will feel flattered that you trust them enough to share with them and this will further strengthen your bond with that person.

If you are finding it difficult to avoid a stressful situation, then you should go for a better alternative which is altering it and this means changing the way you communicate and operate in your daily life. First, you can try by expressing your feelings instead of bottling them up. If someone is trying to bother you, you should try to be more assertive and communicate your concerns in an open and respectful way. If you don't, you will only be piling up stress and resentment which won't make you productive in any way. Also, learn to manage your time better, if you are able to plan ahead, you will feel less stressed when executing your tasks and also find it easier to stay calm and focused.

Sometimes, it is just best to make the time for fun and relaxation, if you regularly take the time to have fun and relax, you will feel less stressful. You must learn to avoid getting caught up in all the distractions, hustle and bustle that life brings with it so much so that you forget to take care of yourself and nurture your mind. Therefore, every day, learn to engage in an activity that brings you joy, make the time for leisure. It could be a mundane thing like looking at the skies or fixing your bike or writing for your blog. You must also work to preserve your sense of humor. No one wants to hang around someone who is moody and angry all the time.

DAY 29:

BE A BETTER LEADER

In your career or personal life, leadership skills matter. Good leadership involves, taking some level of responsibilities for other people and even their shortcomings and failures. For example, the role a father plays in the family as the provider of finances and security and the role of a shift supervisor at a production company.

To become a better version of yourself, you must be able to improve your ability at leading yourself and others. You must be deliberate about your growth; looking at the areas where you have shortcomings and working on them so you can be extremely better and in turn find satisfaction and happiness.

As a leader in your workplace, it is your duty to be able to motivate other employees towards achieving the common goals. Being able to provide inspiration for your team means painting a clearer picture of what success looks like for everybody. And if you are an employee, don't be afraid to ask questions when you hit a grey patch. Speak openly and honestly and give praise when someone deserves it. This makes you visible and also makes people want to connect with you more.

To be a better leader, you must learn to work with people. Understand their stories; their strength, their weakness. Let your intuition guide you in helping and supporting others. Know when and how you should draw people out of their shell to be more useful and make them feel valued for their efforts and contribution.

You can't be a leader if you don't do enough work on your courage, esteem and confidence. Thankfully, how to go about doing this has been previously discussed. You must learn to create an aura of confidence, make decisions in a timely fashion and be unafraid of taking reasonable risk. All these cannot happen if you happen to have feelings of doubt about your abilities or you are feeling inadequate.

To qualify as a good leader, you must be trustworthy and learn to have a faith in others, that they will come through. You must be honest and transparent and stick to your word even if circumstances change and it becomes a bit difficult to deliver on your earlier promise. To be able to do this, you must be in touch with your inner, real self. Identifying your talents and your shortcomings are very important in the path to authenticity. You must be aware of your own strength and weakness and acknowledge that there is more you still need to know, in that way, people will be more likely to extend their offer to help.

As we already know that things change in life, expect that sometimes things may not always work well according to how you and your followers have planned them. You may feel disheartened and things may look very bleak. As the leader of the group, you must be able to stay positive. This doesn't mean you should always see things through rose-colored glasses. It only means that you must be able to keep up a sense of optimism and hope even in the face of challenges.

Finally, you should understand that leadership is not a one-way relationship. As you work towards improving yourself, you must ask for feedback from people who are close to you. This will enable you to gauge your achievement so far with your ultimate goal and keep things in a better perspective for you. You should pay specific attention to things that have been effective in the past and always be on the lookout for new ways to inspire, motivate, and reward yourself and the people you are leading.

DAY 30:

CELEBRATE YOUR VICTORIES TRANSFORMING YOURSELF

If we don't celebrate the little challenges we've overcome and the small victories we've won in life, how do we feel the inspiration to move towards achieving the big ones?

Life hands us a multitude of challenges on a regular; in business, family, marriage, etc. The knowledge that life is a marathon and not a sprint even makes this worse as it makes us realize that setbacks will always happen along the way no matter how intelligent or prayerful we are. A lot of the times, these challenges are out of our control and they tend to weigh us down. Naturally, we tend to ponder and focus so much on these problems that we often fail to realize that we are winning in other ways and thus should celebrate those moments as this can help create new surges of motivation that we so desperately need. But instead of waiting till you have achieved that grand plan of yours, here are reasons to get you started on celebrating the little milestones in your path to transform yourself.

First of all, as said earlier, it gives you the motivation to keep going on in the face of adversity. To be candid, if you take a good look at your life right now, you will discover that there are numerous areas you need to improve on and aren't really where you should be and if you allow yourself to dwell on the shortcomings then you just might give up. When you allow yourself to celebrate how far you have come, you are actually reminding yourself that "I am successful... I'm on the right path..." This will keep your spirits up and give you the boost you need to keep moving on.

Celebrating your victories help build your confidence. If you allow your attention to be focused on every challenge you face, it's very easy to feel your confidence deflated which in turn makes you powerless. But when you celebrate your victories, you make another deposit in your confidence bank that says "I can do this." Confidence is very important because, even if you may have all of the ability in the world to perform well, but you don't believe you have that ability, then you won't perform up to that ability.

Don't bite off more than what you can chew when it comes to goals. Every big goal is accomplished in little stages. If you want to succeed and really enjoy the process to getting there, you will need to break it into smaller and more measurable tasks. Creating small incremental milestones as part of a bigger objective will help you track your progress and keep you moving in the right direction.

Learning to acknowledge yourself for the work you are putting towards your goal helps refresh your brain and keeps you celebrating along the way. We all need encouragement to succeed and celebrating small goals are very effective ways of doing that.

Finally, don't forget to celebrate with others. It is normal for you to descend into feelings of inadequacy and some other negative emotions but it isn't OK. The way to ensure that you put yourself on the right path to accomplishing what you want in your life is to celebrate it in the life of others. The truth is that you can't attract what you resent. Try your best to capitalize on what you had learned on this "Thirty Days to Transform Yourself" journey. Keep on repeating the methods until they become the norm for your success. Congratulations!!

ABOUT THE AUTHOR

Dr. Iona German, PhD is also the Author and Editor of "You and Your True Self" and "A Healthy Happier You." She teaches seminars worldwide on empowering yourself. She was educated at the University of the West Indies, Jamaica, Pittman's Institute, England and in the USA. A Motivational Speaker, Counselor, Professor and Entrepreneur. A woman of many talents helping people to accomplish their goals, dreams and aspirations.

www.ingramcontent.com/pod-product-compliance
Lightning Source LLC
Chambersburg PA
CBHW070501100426
42743CB00010B/1720
```
*9 780997 768206*
```